ON THE FLAVOUR TRAIL

VANCOUVER ISLAND TAMALES

FOOD FEST AT HISTORIC FORT RODD HILL

On the Flavour TRAIL

RECIPES BY ISLAND CHEFS' COLLABORATIVE
EDITED BY CHRISTABEL PADMORE

TouchWood
Editions

TouchWood Editions
touchwoodeditions.com

LIBRARY AND ARCHIVES CANADA CATALOGUING IN PUBLICATION
On the flavour trail / Island Chefs' Collaborative ;
Christabel Padmore, editor.

Includes index.
Issued also in electronic formats.
ISBN 978-1-77151-006-6

1. Cooking, Canadian—British Columbia style.
2. Cooking—British Columbia—Vancouver Island.
3. Cookbooks. I. Padmore, Christabel II. Island Chefs'
Collaborative

TX715.6.O538 2013   641.59711'2   C2012-908108-6

Editor: Holland Gidney
Cover images: Maryanne Carmack
Interior photos: Maryanne Carmack except page 121 Rafael Laguillo, istockphoto.com
Design: Pete Kohut

We gratefully acknowledge the financial support for our publishing activities
from the Government of Canada through the Canada Book Fund, Canada
Council for the Arts, and the province of British Columbia through the
British Columbia Arts Council and the Book Publishing Tax Credit.

This book was produced using FSC®-certified, acid-free paper,
processed chlorine free and printed with soya-based inks.

1 2 3 4 5 17 16 15 14 13

PRINTED IN CHINA

For our farmers

CONTENTS

LOCALLY INSPIRED WOOD-FIRED PIZZA

INTRODUCTION

Founded in early 1999, the Island Chefs' Collaborative (ICC) is a community-based, non-profit organization dedicated to creating and preserving sustainable local food and agriculture on Vancouver Island and the Gulf Islands. We are like-minded chefs and food and beverage professionals with a common interest in regional food security, the preservation of farmland and the development of local food systems.

Over the years, the ICC has raised more than two hundred thousand dollars to support numerous community groups and new farms in our region. Similarly, our chef members purchase produce directly from local farms, amounting to thousands of dollars each year in revenue for farmers. Our fundraising events, such as the annual Island Chefs' Food Fest, have become highlights of Vancouver Island's festival season. Chefs from some of the finest restaurants on the West Coast are working together to raise public awareness of local

sustainability issues and support for locally produced food. Collaboration is key: teaming up with other community groups, like LifeCycles' Fruit Tree Project (see page 57), only brings us closer to our goal of urban sustainability and food security. Similarly, the ICC has partnered with FarmFolk CityFolk and VanCity to offer one hundred thousand dollars in zero-interest microloans to farmers and food processors. Funds raised by the ICC go towards supporting the administration of and interest rebates for the loans.

This cookbook is a project close to our hearts. As chefs, we believe food should be nourishing but also, and above all, delicious. This book demonstrates that ingredients need not traverse the globe for food to taste rich and exotic. Our contributors have used the very best local and sustainable ingredients to create a collection of recipes that will keep you cooking close to home throughout the seasons. The recipes in this book have been developed, tested and tasted by the local food community and we have worked hard to elevate the beautiful flavours of the region to gourmet heights. Eating local has never tasted so indulgent.

Thank you so much for supporting the ICC by choosing this book. We are always looking for new members and volunteers to help contribute and assist us in achieving our goals. If you are interested in learning more about how you can get involved with the ICC, please visit our website at iccbc.ca.

Island Chefs' Collaborative

SHUCKING STATION

TOULOUSE SAUSAGE - HEIRLOOM PORK

FOREWORD

Chefs—sometimes they're a weird lot. But if you shared their working conditions, you might end up a little weird as well. They work sixteen hours a day sometimes, most often at night, even on weekends and holidays, in hot, sweaty kitchens full of deadlines and demands. And then they fall exhausted into bed, only to wake up a few hours later to do it all over again.

The chefs contributing to this cookbook are not Food Network stars or "celebrity" chefs. They are the people who labour in the kitchens of Vancouver Island restaurants, catering companies and cooking classrooms, bringing you the best their skills have to offer in combination with the best ingredients this island has to offer.

And Vancouver Island does have a lot to offer. As you page your way through this cookbook, you will find recipes that take advantage of what we have here. Our food culture is drawn from the land and the ocean. Seafood like salmon, shrimp and crab, halibut, clams and oysters. On land, more farmers than ever are raising heritage breeds of pigs, lamb, cattle and goats, and island chefs are re-introducing this heritage, slowly but surely, to their menus. And, thanks to very fertile grasslands on southern Vancouver Island, our farmers grow excellent fruits and vegetables and produce high-quality milk and dairy products.

These farmers are part of the reason the Island Chefs' Collaborative was formed. The co-operation started slowly, with chefs and farmers getting together once a year to plot strategy for the coming planting season. It made sense: why shouldn't farmers grow what chefs wanted to serve in their restaurants? Why shouldn't chefs commit to a product a farmer will grow specifically for them? And then the fundraising started. With more chefs getting out of their kitchens and visiting farms, they gleaned a greater realization of how difficult farming can be—and how a little bit of financial support can go a long way. How a proper fence could save thousands of dollars of produce from being gobbled up by those ubiquitous hungry deer. How a drip irrigation system could save a farmer hours of time spent watering and use an important resource more sparingly.

Now that the initial grants program has morphed into a microloan fund allowing farmers and producers to apply for small loans with an interest rebate to the recipient when the loan is paid off. These rebates are made possible by the fundraising efforts of the Island Chefs' Collaborative.

And that fundraising is made possible by those busy chefs giving up even more of their precious time off to take part in events like their biggest splash, the ICC Food Fest at Fort Rodd Hill, held every June. The chefs bring the food, the public brings their appetites. And everyone leaves with a smile on their face.

One of the main goals of the Island Chefs' Collaborative is to promote a sustainable food and agriculture system. Chefs are trend leaders: what happens in their kitchens and dining rooms is often reflected down the line in home kitchens and family meals. We can see the ICC chefs are making a difference: people are asking questions about where their food comes from and how it is produced. Count the number of farmers' markets on Vancouver Island: there are so many more now than there were even just ten years ago—and they're popping up everywhere. So many families are joining Community Supported Agriculture (CSA) programs that some farmers have had to start waiting lists.

Like I mentioned before, being a chef can get a little weird. It's one of those professions where you don't necessarily move up the chain of command by staying with the same company. Chefs move around. By the time a young chef hits twenty-five, he or she may have already worked at a dozen different restaurants—and may have also done some travelling to work for free for a famous chef or at a restaurant known around the world in order to garner some valuable experience. What a chef might lose in job security or stability is offset by what he or she gains in camaraderie, connections and skills. On Vancouver Island, you need only look to the Sooke Harbour House to see how a commitment to local and sustainable eating has influenced a whole generation of chefs who have worked there at one time or another. Many of them have since started their own restaurants, sharing much of the same local and seasonal philosophy of Sooke Harbour House owners Sinclair and Frédérique Philip—and in turn they pass that philosophy on to their employees, and so on and so on.

When I look at the recipes in this cookbook, it's easy to see how the ICC chefs love to use the ingredients of the region and that they are generously passing on their specialties to you. Farm, forest, field, orchard and sea are all well represented with some of Vancouver Island's favourite ingredients: Dungeness crab, scallops and spot prawns; wild mushrooms, stinging nettles and nodding onions; hazelnuts, blueberries and apples; lamb, chicken, duck and pork—and more.

I've been living on the West Coast for nearly twenty years now, and I am continually amazed at the creativity, ingenuity and drive of the many chefs I've had the great fortune to meet. Without exception they have always been generous with their time and their knowledge and, above all, their willingness to take part in fundraising efforts that protect, defend and promote the farmers, fishers, foragers and producers who provide the excellent ingredients they use towards achieving their daily goal of pleasing our palates. I hope that when you are trying the recipes in this cookbook, you will think about where your food comes from and, whenever possible, try to support your local producers, who work so hard to help you enjoy the bounty of Vancouver Island, straight from their farm or shop to your kitchen.

Don Genova

SEA ANGELS

SEA

Crab and Rockfish Cakes with Caper, Red Onion and Preserved Lemon Aïoli

COSMO MEENS

YIELD: 30 cakes

Cakes

1 cup (250 mL) finely diced orange pepper
1 cup (250 mL) finely diced yellow pepper
1 cup (250 mL) finely diced red pepper
1 cup (250 mL) finely diced green onion
1 cup (250 mL) finely diced celery
1 lb (500 g) skinless, boneless
    rockfish fillets
1 lb (500 g) crab meat
1 cup (250 mL) mayonnaise
½ cup (125 mL) grainy mustard
10 cranks freshly ground black pepper
1–2 tsp (5–10 mL) sea salt

Breading

6 eggs
½ cup (125 mL) water
all-purpose flour
14 oz (400 g) box Panko
    (Japanese) breadcrumbs
olive oil, for frying

In a frying pan, sauté peppers, onion and celery until slightly caramelized. And then dice rockfish fillets. Squeeze excess liquid from crab meat. Mix all ingredients together, adding just enough mayo and mustard to moisten but not make soggy. Make 30 golfball-sized cakes, then place on a tray and refrigerate for about 20 minutes to set a bit. Meanwhile, prepare breading station with three bowls.

Whisk eggs with water and place in 1 bowl. Place Panko and plain flour in 2 separate bowls.

When ready, remove cakes from fridge. Warm some olive oil in a frying pan and begin to coat the cakes. First dredge in flour, dusting off any excess. Then dip in egg wash. Finally coat in Panko and fry in some olive oil. Keep the oil handy because cakes will soak up quite a bit. Fry and place on an ungreased tray and bake in a 300°F (150°C) oven for 15 minutes. Serve with Caper, Red Onion and Preserved Lemon Aïoli and some fresh parsley.

Caper, Red Onion and Preserved Lemon Aïoli

In a food processor, blend eggs, egg yolks, grainy Dijon, lemon juice, garlic, honey and salt. Slowly add oil in a steady stream until mixture is thick and emulsified. Stir in remaining ingredients and place in fridge until ready to serve.

Aïoli

2 eggs

2 egg yolks

1 Tbsp (15 mL) grainy Dijon mustard

3 Tbsp (45 mL) lemon juice

1 Tbsp (15 mL) chopped garlic

1 Tbsp (15 mL) honey

1 Tbsp (15 mL) sea salt

¾ cup (185 mL) olive oil (or other oil of your choice)

¼ cup (60 mL) finely diced onion

¼ cup (60 mL) chopped capers

2 Tbsp (30 mL) minced preserved lemon rind

2 Tbsp (30 mL) chopped fresh dill (optional)

Dungeness Crab Stuffed Morels

DWANE MACISAAC

YIELD: 4 servings

2 cups (500 mL) chicken stock
3 oz (100 g) large dried morel mushrooms
7 oz (200 g) fresh Dungeness crab meat
juice and zest of 1 lemon, divided
fresh thyme, to taste
ground pepper, to taste
1 Tbsp (15 mL) butter
¼ cup (60 mL) dry white wine

In a medium saucepan, simmer stock and morels for 10 minutes. Drain mushrooms, reserving liquid. Lay mushrooms on a kitchen towel to dry. Check crab meat for any shell bits and then chop finely. Place in a bowl and add lemon juice, thyme and ground pepper. Stuff the mixture into each mushroom and then sauté in a medium-hot sauté pan with butter and lemon zest. Remove mushrooms and place in a warm oven. Deglaze the pan with white wine and reserved chicken stock. Reduce liquid for 10 minutes to make a sauce for morels.

DUNGENESS CRAB "EN PAPILLOTE"

Gravlax with West Coast Hemp Vodka

DWANE MACISAAC

YIELD: 20–24 servings

2 whole sides of salmon (about 5 lb
    [2.2 kg] each), deboned, skin on
¼ cup (60 mL) kosher salt
¼ cup (60 mL) white sugar
2 Tbsp (30 mL) white peppercorns, crushed
2 bunches fresh dill
½ cup (125 mL) Left Coast Hemp Vodka

Line a glass dish large enough to hold one salmon side with plastic wrap. Lay one side, skin side down, on the plastic wrap.

Mix salt, sugar and crushed peppercorns in a bowl and then spread half this cure mix over surface of fillet. Lay whole fresh dill overtop. Sprinkle vodka over the dill. Spread remainder of cure mix over dill and top with second side of salmon, skin side up.

Pull plastic wrap up to cover fillets. Place a dish or some plates on top of salmon and weigh it down using canned food or other heavy items.

Place the dish in the refrigerator for 48–72 hours. Once or twice a day, remove the dish, unwrap salmon and baste it with any juices that have accumulated. Flip fish over and return the dish to the refrigerator.

To serve, remove fillets from their wrapping, remove dill and scrape off any excess cure mix. Slice thinly on the bias and serve with artisan breads, crème fraîche and a crisp white wine or Prosecco.

Grilled Albacore Tuna Salad "West Coast"

JOHN WALLER

YIELD: 2 servings

Place tuna loin in a bowl with olive oil, balsamic vinegar, lemon juice, zest, and salt and pepper. Set aside.

Lightly toast quinoa in a cooking pot, then add olive oil, garlic, shallot, chili flakes and fennel seeds. Add 1½ cups (375 mL) cold water and ¼ teaspoon (1 mL) salt. Bring to a boil, then cover with a tight-fitting lid and turn the heat down to simmer. Cook for 15 minutes. Remove quinoa from heat and allow to sit for 5 minutes with the lid on. Fluff quinoa *gently* with a fork, add fennel, dill, tomatoes, basil and parsley, then dress with lemon juice, olive oil and salt and pepper to taste. Set aside.

On a preheated barbecue, grill the tuna for 1 minute on each side. Slice and serve overtop quinoa salad.

Tuna

5 oz (150 g) Albacore tuna loin
1 Tbsp (15 mL) olive oil
2 Tbsp (30 mL) balsamic vinegar
juice and zest of 1 lemon
salt and freshly ground black pepper

Quinoa Salad

1 cup (250 mL) quinoa
1 Tbsp (15 mL) olive oil
1 garlic clove, minced
1 shallot, minced
pinch of chili flakes
pinch of fennel seeds
¼ tsp (1 mL) salt
¼ cup (60 mL) shaved fennel bulb
1 Tbsp (15 mL) fresh dill, minced
½ cup (125 mL) cherry tomatoes, sliced
1 Tbsp (15 mL) fresh basil, chopped
1 Tbsp (15 mL) fresh parsley, chopped
juice of 1 lemon
splash of olive oil
salt and pepper, to taste

Halibut and Clams with Peas and Parsley

CHRISTABEL PADMORE

YIELD: 4 servings

vegetable oil, for frying

½ medium white onion, sliced

1 shallot, minced

1 small fennel bulb, finely sliced

¼ tsp (1 mL) espellette chili powder
   (substitute another red chili if
   espellette is unavailable)

1 Tbsp (15 mL) smoked sweet paprika

1 tsp (5 mL) fennel seeds,
   toasted and then ground

2 cups (500 mL) seafood stock
   (or use vegetable or chicken stock,
   and use unsalted butter if it is
   a commercial stock or base)

1 cup (250 mL) dry white wine

4–5 oz (150 g) fresh halibut fillets

1 cup (250 mL) all-purpose flour

salt and pepper, to taste

¼ cup (60 mL) salted butter

20 medium butter or manila clams, rinsed

2 cups (500 mL) fresh or frozen peas

1 bunch fresh parsley, chopped

Add a small amount of vegetable oil to a medium-sized saucepan on high heat, then add onion, shallot and fennel. Sauté until onion is translucent. Add chili powder, smoked paprika and ground fennel. Stir, then add the stock and wine. Stir and bring to a simmer. Trim any skin off halibut and portion the fish. Pour flour onto a plate and season with salt and pepper.

Dredge halibut in seasoned flour. In an oven-safe frying pan, add 2 tablespoons (30 mL) vegetable oil and raise to high heat. Add fillets and sear until golden brown. Remove from heat and place in a 375°F (190°C) oven for 5–10 minutes, depending on thickness of fillets.

Add butter and clams to the broth (if clams are sandy, cook separately, and add to broth once cooked). When clams start to open, add in peas and parsley and simmer until all the clams are open (discard any clams that haven't opened after approximately 5 minutes of cooking). Season with salt and pepper, as necessary.

Ladle broth and clams into soup plates and place cooked halibut in the centre.

Serve with fresh baguette or croutons and a hot-weather white wine.

SHUCKED SEA ANGEL

Oysters with Shallot Mignonette

PATRICK SIMPSON

YIELD: 12 pieces

Mignonette

1 shallot, finely minced

1 Tbsp (15 mL) white wine

1 Tbsp (15 mL) red wine vinegar

1 tsp (5 mL) white sugar

salt and pepper, to taste

**12 fresh small oysters from
    a reputable fishmonger**

Combine all mignonette ingredients in a bowl and stir until sugar has dissolved. Cover and refrigerate for 2–24 hours.

Shuck oysters and serve immediately with a drizzle of mignonette over each one.

Porcini Crusted Halibut

DWANE MACISAAC

YIELD: 4 servings

Preheat oven to 400°F (200°C).

In a blender (or dedicated spice grinder), buzz porcinis until they're dust. Brush halibut portions with half of the olive oil and then dredge in the porcini powder. Add remaining olive oil to a medium-hot sauté pan and lightly brown the halibut on all sides. Add salt and pepper and lemon zest and place in oven for 10–15 minutes.

Serve with dauphinoise (scalloped) potatoes.

4–6 oz (175 g) portions fresh halibut

2 Tbsp (30 mL) olive oil, divided

3 oz (90 g) dried porcini mushrooms (or use mushroom powder)

sea salt and ground pepper, to taste

zest of 1 lemon

FIRE-ROASTING LOCAL SQUID

Pumpkin and Side Stripe Shrimp Stuffed Phyllo Parcels

COSMO MEENS

YIELD: 4 servings

1 cup (250 mL) onion, diced

¼ cup (60 mL) garlic, chopped

2 Tbsp (30 mL) toasted sesame oil

2 Tbsp (30 mL) sambal oelek
(or substitute fresh red Thai
chilies with seeds removed)

4 cups (1 L) medium-large squash
or pumpkin, peeled and diced

1½ cups (375 mL) Thai basil leaves,
chopped

30 oz (900 mL) coconut milk

10½ oz (300 g) fresh or frozen
side stripe shrimp

3 Tbsp (45 mL) fermented soybeans
(or use miso paste)

1 Tbsp (15 mL) Bragg's
(or substitute soy sauce)

2 Tbsp (30 mL) honey or palm sugar

¾ lb (350 g) butter

1 package organic spelt (or regular)
phyllo pastry

Sauté onions and garlic in sesame oil. Add sambal oelek (or chilies). Then add squash and basil. Stir it all up, then add coconut milk. Let mixture simmer and peel (thawed) shrimp. Squash is cooked when a piece can be squished against the side of the pot with a fork. Once the squash is cooked, strain out all the chunks from the sauce and set aside in a baking dish to cool, reserving the liquid.

Return liquid to a saucepan, add fermented soybeans, Bragg's, and honey or sugar, and reduce by half or a third. Once sauce is reduced, do a final seasoning, adding just the right amount of salt and sugar to get it exactly how you want it to taste. Once the squash that was strained out of the sauce is cooled, stir in raw shrimp and enough reduced liquid to just coat everything but not pool in the dish.

Melt butter in a small saucepan. Remove phyllo pastry from box and roll out flat on a clean surface. Use a damp tea towel to cover the dough sheets that are not being worked on. Lay one sheet on a work surface and use a pastry brush to completely cover it with melted butter. Then lay another sheet on top and repeat a third time. Brush the final layer with butter, then cut the large sheet into 4 equal rectangles. Place ¼–½ cup (60–125 mL) of the pumpkin prawn filling in the centre of each rectangle, making sure edges can be folded over the filling to meet in the middle. Fold the sides over the filling, brushing all surfaces of the dough with butter as you fold. Fold end to end, brushing with butter as well. Brush the top and the bottom of the parcel with butter and set aside on a baking tray.

In an oven preheated to 400°F (200°C), bake parcels for about 35 minutes, or until their tops are a nice golden brown. (Premade parcels can also be refrigerated for a few hours before baking.) Serve with a drizzle of remaining coconut reduction.

Sablefish with Grilled Seaweed and Miso Green Tea

DWANE MACISAAC

YIELD: 4 servings

1 tsp (5 mL) grated fresh ginger

2 Tbsp (30 mL) miso paste

4–6 oz (175 mL) portions sablefish
    (Black cod)

1 Tbsp (15 mL) loose green tea

4 fresh shiso leaves (available
    at Japanese grocery stores)

olive oil, for frying

3 oz (90 g) fresh seaweed (or 2 oz
    [60 g] if using dried)

1 oz (30 g) daikon radish sprouts

Mix ginger and miso and rub onto each portion of fish. Boil 2 cups (500 mL) water. Add green tea and shiso leaves to a teapot. Add boiling water and steep for 2–3 minutes.

In a medium-hot sauté pan, add a little olive oil and sauté fish for 1 minute per side, then finish in a 350°F (180°C) oven for 10 minutes. On a grill plate or charbroiler, grill seaweed for garnish. Place grilled seaweed in a bowl, add the fish, then pour strained tea overtop and garnish with a chiffonade of shiso and a pinch of daikon sprouts.

Salmon Cakes

GARRETT SCHACK

YIELD: 4 servings

Place onion, garlic and dill in a food processor. Blend until onions and dill are very fine. Combine these ingredients in a large bowl with salmon, lemon zest and juice, egg, breadcrumbs, capers, and salt and pepper. Mix well. Form mixture into 8 even-sized patties (2 per person).

Preheat a flat-bottomed pan to medium and then add a thin coating of oil. Fry patties for 2–3 minutes each side or until golden brown. Serve with some fresh organic greens and a favourite dipping sauce.

1 small onion, chopped

1 clove garlic, minced

1 cup (250 mL) fresh dill (a large handful)

1 lb (500 g) fresh pink salmon, skinned, boned and coarsely chopped in a food processor

zest of 1 lemon

juice of ½ a lemon

1 egg

1 cup (250 mL) dry breadcrumbs

2 Tbsp (30 mL) capers

salt and pepper, to taste

vegetable or olive oil, for frying

WEST COAST BOUNTY

Salmon Pastrami

MICHAEL PAGNACCO

YIELD: 10–12 servings

Combine all the brine ingredients in a saucepan and bring to a boil. Set aside and allow to cool. Place salmon in a baking dish and pour cooled brine overtop. Cover and refrigerate for 48 hours.

Remove salmon from brine and rinse under cool water. Towel dry fillet, then cold smoke in a smoker on wire racks for 20 minutes. Refrigerate smoked salmon uncovered for 4 hours.

Toast spice mixture ingredients (except molasses) in a frying pan.

Brush salmon lightly with molasses and dust with spice mixture.

Serve with rye bread crostini, capers and thinly sliced red onion.

Brine

1 cup (250 mL) demerara brown sugar
¼ cup (60 mL) kosher salt
4 cups (1 L) water
1 bay leaf
1 tsp (5 mL) mustard seeds
1 Tbsp (15 mL) coriander seeds
1 tsp (5 mL) black peppercorns
4–6 lb (2–3 kg) salmon fillet,
    skin on, scales removed

Spice Mixture

2 Tbsp (30 mL) coriander seeds, ground
1 Tbsp (15 mL) mustard seeds, ground
1 Tbsp (15 mL) black peppercorns, ground
1 tsp (5 mL) allspice, ground
1 Tbsp (15 mL) paprika
¼ tsp (1 mL) cayenne pepper
½ cup (125 mL) molasses

Scallops with Brown Butter and Capers

PATRICK SIMPSON

YIELD: 4 servings, as a first course

12 large scallops
sea salt and black pepper, to taste
¼ cup (60 mL) olive oil
3 Tbsp (45 mL) unsalted butter
1 Tbsp (15 mL) shallot, minced
2 Tbsp (30 mL) capers, rinsed
juice of ½ a lemon
⅓ cup (80 mL) flat-leaf
    parsley, finely chopped

Pat scallops dry with paper towels, then season lightly with salt and pepper. Heat a large sauté pan or non-reactive frying pan over medium-high and add oil. Allow oil to warm, then add scallops. Do not crowd scallops in the pan. Sauté until well seared, about 2 minutes per side. Transfer scallops to a plate, cover and keep warm.

Add butter to the sauté pan and cook until it begins to foam and turn golden. Add shallots and capers, then sauté for 1 minute. Add lemon juice and parsley.

To serve, place scallops on warmed plates. Spoon butter, shallots and capers overtop.

GOOSENECK BARNACLES

Sea Urchins with Lemon and Olive Oil

CHRISTABEL PADMORE

YIELD: 4 servings, as a first course

Wearing rubber gloves and using scissors, cut around the base of each sea urchin in a circular direction. Remove liquid and viscera and discard. Delicately remove roe attached to the shell and reserve. Repeat for other urchins.

Clean the urchin shells. Carefully return roe to the shells. Drizzle with olive oil, lemon juice and salt. Serve.

12 sea urchins
2 Tbsp (30 mL) extra-virgin olive oil
juice of 1 lemon
pinch of sea salt

Side Stripe Shrimp and Halibut Cheek Salad

COSMO MEENS

YIELD: 4–6 servings

½ cup (125 mL) lime juice

3 Tbsp (45 mL) fish sauce

2–3 fresh lemongrass stalks
(white part only), finely sliced

15 fresh lime leaves, finely shredded

1 tsp (5 mL) roasted chili powder

1 lb (500 g) halibut cheeks

1 lb (500 g) side stripe shrimp

3 Tbsp (45 mL) toasted jasmine rice powder

5 oz (150 g) Asian shallots
(or substitute regular shallots)

½ cup (125 mL) fresh mint leaves

lettuce leaves and cabbage or other
fresh greens, for garnishing

In a small saucepan, bring lime juice and fish sauce to a boil and reduce. Add lemongrass, lime leaves and chili powder. Add halibut cheeks and cook until they can be shredded with a fork. Add side stripe shrimp and cook for about 1–2 minutes. Strain off any excess liquid, then add toasted rice powder and shallots. Stir together. A small amount of the liquid that was poured off can be added back, but only enough so that none is pooling at the bottom. Serve with freshly torn mint leaves and fresh lettuce or cabbage leaves for garnish.

Snapper Ceviche

MATT RISSLING

YIELD: 4–6 servings

Combine all ingredients and then refrigerate for at least 4 hours, or overnight.

    Serve with tortilla chips.

1 lb (500 g) snapper fillet, diced

1 cup (250 mL) lime juice

zest of 1 lime

½ cup (125 mL) lemon juice

½ cup (125 mL) orange juice

2 shallots, minced

2 Tbsp (30 mL) fresh flat-leaf
    parsley, chopped

¼ cup (60 mL) white wine vinegar

½ tsp (2 mL) sambal oelek

salt and pepper, to taste

SARDINES

Thai-Flavoured Spot Prawn Bisque

BILL JONES

YIELD: 6–8 servings

Peel prawns, reserving shells, and place in a shallow metal or glass tray. Sprinkle lightly with salt and sugar. Cover with boiling water and let sit for 5 minutes before draining and chilling.

Place prawn shells on a baking tray and place in a 350°F (175°C) oven. Roast shells for 15 minutes, or until they have lightly browned. In a stockpot, add a little oil and then the onion, carrot and celery. Sauté until they begin to brown, then add 8 cups (2 L) water and bring to a simmer. Add the prawns shells, ginger slices, lemongrass, cilantro stems, lime juice and zest, and coconut milk. Bring to a boil, then reduce heat and simmer for 1 hour.

Strain soup, check seasoning and adjust with salt and pepper (or hot sauce if you like it spicy). Mix the cornstarch with 2 tablespoons (30 mL) cold water and then slowly whisk into the hot soup. The mixture will thicken as it heats. Before serving, stir in the cilantro leaves and cooked prawns. Serve immediately.

1 lb (500 g) spot prawns

1 Tbsp (15 mL) salt

1 tsp (5 mL) white sugar

oil, for frying

1 large onion, peeled and chopped

2 large carrots, peeled and chopped

1 stalk celery, chopped

4 slices fresh ginger

1 bulb garlic, peeled and chopped

1 stalk fresh lemongrass, trimmed
    and cut into chunks

1 bunch fresh cilantro, divided
    into stalks and stems

juice and zest of 1 lime

10-oz (300 mL) can coconut milk

salt and pepper, to taste

hot sauce (optional)

2 Tbsp (30 mL) cornstarch

fresh cilantro (or basil) leaves, for garnishing

HARBOUR HOUSE ORGANIC FARM ~ SALT SPRING ISLAND

ORCHARD

FRY'S RED WHEAT BREAD

Apple and Blueberry Cake

BILL JONES

YIELD: 6–8 servings

Preheat the oven to 375°F (190°C) and grease a 12-inch (20 cm) round cake pan or 13 × 9-inch (3.5 L) baking pan, then dust it with flour.

In a large mixing bowl, cream together butter and sugar until smooth. Add one egg at a time, mixing until incorporated. Stir in sour cream and vanilla and mix until smooth.

In a medium mixing bowl, stir together flour and baking powder. Add the dry ingredients to the wet ingredients in two or three batches, stirring until just mixed and being careful not to overwork the batter.

Gently fold chopped apples and blueberries into the batter and pour the batter into the prepared pan. Bake for 45–60 minutes, until a toothpick inserted into the centre of the cake comes out clean.

Transfer to a cooling rack and serve warm, or at room temperature, with ice cream.

Variations
Add 1 tablespoon (15 mL) chopped fresh rosemary.
Add 1 teaspoon (5 mL) cinnamon instead of vanilla.
Use blackberries instead of blueberries.

½ cup (125 mL) butter (or olive oil)

1 cup (250 mL) brown sugar

3 eggs

½ cup (125 mL) sour cream

1 tsp (5 mL) vanilla

2½ cups (625 mL) flour

2 tsp (10 mL) baking powder

2 cups (500 mL) Cowichan apples, cored, peeled and chopped

2 cups (500 mL) blueberries, fresh or frozen

Berkshire Bacon and Blue Cheese Caramelized Pear Salad with Local Greens

DWANE MACISAAC

YIELD: 6 servings

4 Tbsp (60 mL) olive oil

1 Tbsp (15 mL) freshly
squeezed lemon juice

1 tsp (5 mL) white wine vinegar

1¼ tsp (6 mL) Dijon or whole-grain
prepared mustard

3 Tbsp (45 mL) butter

¼–½ tsp (1–2 mL) maple syrup or honey

2 tsp (10 mL) finely minced green onions
(white and light green parts only)

sea salt and ground pepper, to taste

3 Bartlett pears, peeled, cored and
sliced into very thin wedges

6 slices of bacon (preferably Berkshire)

½ pound (250 g) fresh local greens

4 oz (125 g) blue cheese, crumbled

In a medium mixing bowl or large measuring cup, prepare dressing by whisking together first 4 ingredients until well blended. Set aside.

In a medium frying pan over medium heat, melt butter and stir in maple syrup or honey and pears. Cook for 5–7 minutes, stirring constantly, until the pears are fragrant, caramelized and lightly browned. Transfer pears to a plate and set aside, returning the pan to medium heat. Using the same pan, cook the bacon to desired crispness. Remove from heat and crumble or slice into bite-size pieces once cool.

Place greens in a large salad bowl and add the pears, cheese and cooked bacon. Drizzle with dressing and toss gently to distribute ingredients evenly. Serve immediately.

Buttermilk Beignets with Caramel Apples and Rosemary

TARA BLACK

YIELD: 20 beignets and sauce

In a large mixing bowl, combine flour, baking soda, baking powder and sugar and mix well. In a medium mixing bowl, beat together buttermilk and egg. Add the wet ingredients to the dry ingredients and stir to form a smooth batter.

Heat 3 inches (8 cm) of peanut oil in a heavy-bottomed pot until it reaches 375°F (190°C). Using two tablespoons, drop dollops of batter into the oil and gently fry the donuts until golden all over, turning occasionally to make sure they are evenly cooked. Using a slotted spoon, remove donuts from oil and drain on paper towels. Spread cinnamon sugar on a plate and roll warm donuts in it until coated. Set aside and prepare the caramel.

In a medium saucepan over medium heat, add the sugar to the water. Stirring constantly, cook until an amber-coloured caramel is achieved. Add butter and cream and stir to combine. Remove sauce from heat and add rosemary sprig and let sit for 1 hour. Reheat gently to serve. (Caramel will keep for 1 month refrigerated.)

To serve, place 1 cup (250 mL) warm caramel in a dish alongside roasted apple slices and beignets. Dig in!

Beignets

1 cup (250 mL) all-purpose flour
¼ tsp (1 mL) baking soda
1 tsp (5 mL) baking powder
2 Tbsp (30 mL) sugar
1 cup (250 mL) buttermilk
1 egg
peanut oil, for deep-frying
½ cup (125 mL) sugar mixed with
    1 tsp (5 mL) cinnamon

Caramel

1 Tbsp (15 mL) water
¾ cup (185 mL) sugar
1 Tbsp (15 mL) butter
2 Tbsp (30 mL) heavy cream
1 sprig fresh rosemary
2 apples, sliced and lightly roasted in the
    oven (just enough to brown them)

Paradise Jelly

HEIDI FINK

YIELD: 6 cups (1.5 L)

1½ lb (750 g) ripe quince, including peels and cores, washed and chopped

¾ lb (375 g) apples, including peels and cores, washed and chopped

1–1½ cups (250–375 mL) cranberries, sorted, washed and drained

2–3 cups (500–750 mL) organic sugar

In a 4- to 5-quart (3.5–5 L) saucepan over high heat, add prepared fruit and 5–6 cups (1.25–1.5 L) water. Cover pot and bring water to a quick boil. Uncover pot and simmer for about 30–45 minutes, until apples are mushy and quince is tender. Remove from heat and let cool.

Drip fruit through jelly bag into a large measuring cup to obtain 3–4 cups (750 mL–1 L) of juice. Measure the juice that has been obtained and then measure out ¾ cup (175 mL) of sugar for every 1 cup (250 mL) juice and set aside. (Use less sugar if you are using plain white sugar rather than organic sugar.)

To make jelly, place juice in a saucepan. Bring quickly to a boil and skim off any foam that comes to the surface. Add measured sugar, and bring to a boil again, stirring to dissolve sugar. Boil for about 5 minutes, or until gel tests done. (The easiest way to test this is to drip a teaspoon of juice onto a very cold plate and let it sit for a few seconds. Next, drag your fingers gently across the top of the cold jelly. If the surface of the jelly wrinkles, even if the rest of the jelly seems too liquidy, the jelly is ready.) Be very careful not to overboil the jelly!

Immediately fill hot, sterilized jars to within ¼ inch (6 mm) of the top. Seal and process in boiling water bath for 5 minutes. (You can get away with just putting on the caps and seals and letting them seal themselves as they cool. Jelly is over 50 percent sugar and has no fruit pieces in it, so it won't go bad very easily.)

Pear Bread Pudding with Caramelized Ginger and Butterscotch Sauce

DWANE MACISAAC

YIELD: 8–10 servings

12 oz (375 g) multigrain bread,
  cut into 1-inch (2.5 cm)
  cubes (choose a sturdy loaf)

1 Tbsp (15 mL) unsalted butter, divided

2 Tbsp (30 mL) canola oil, divided

3 large pears, peeled, halved, cored and
  thinly sliced (choose firm yet ripe fruit)

2 pinches of allspice, divided

2¾ cups (685 mL) whipping cream

4 eggs, lightly beaten

3 Tbsp (45 mL) turbinado sugar or firmly
  packed light brown sugar, divided

2 Tbsp (30 mL) dark honey

2 tsp (10 mL) vanilla extract

1 tsp (5 mL) ground cinnamon

2 Tbsp (30 mL) candied ginger, chopped

⅛ tsp (0.5 mL) ground cloves

Preheat the oven to 350°F (180°C). Lightly coat a 9-inch (23 cm) square baking dish with cooking spray.

Arrange bread cubes in a single layer on a greased baking sheet. Bake until lightly toasted, about 5 minutes. Set aside.

In a large, non-stick frying pan, melt 1½ teaspoons (7.5 mL) of the butter over medium heat until frothy. Stir in 1 tablespoon (15 mL) of the canola oil. Add half of the pear slices to the pan and sauté until evenly browned, about 10 minutes. Sprinkle a generous pinch of allspice onto the pears, then transfer them to a plate. Repeat with remaining butter, oil, pears and allspice.

Arrange half of the toasted bread cubes evenly in the bottom of the prepared baking dish. Top with half of the sautéed pears and then the remaining bread cubes.

In a large bowl, combine whipping cream, eggs, 2 tablespoons (30 mL) of the sugar, honey, vanilla, cinnamon, ginger and cloves. Whisk until well blended. Pour the cream mixture over the bread and cover with plastic wrap. Let stand for 20–30 minutes, pressing down gently every so often until the bread absorbs the custard mixture. Remove the plastic wrap and arrange the remaining pears on top. Sprinkle with remaining 1 tablespoon (15 mL) sugar.

Bake until a knife inserted into the centre of the pudding comes out clean, 45–55 minutes.

Butterscotch Sauce

In a medium saucepan over medium heat, bring the brown sugar, butter and golden syrup to a boil. Boil for 3 minutes or until smooth, stirring occasionally. Remove from heat and stir in the vanilla and cream. The sauce will thicken as it cools.

Warm the sauce before serving.

Sauce

1½ cups (375 mL) light
    brown sugar, packed

4 Tbsp (60 mL) unsalted butter

⅓ cup (80 mL) golden syrup

¾ tsp (4 mL) vanilla

½ cup (125 mL) heavy cream

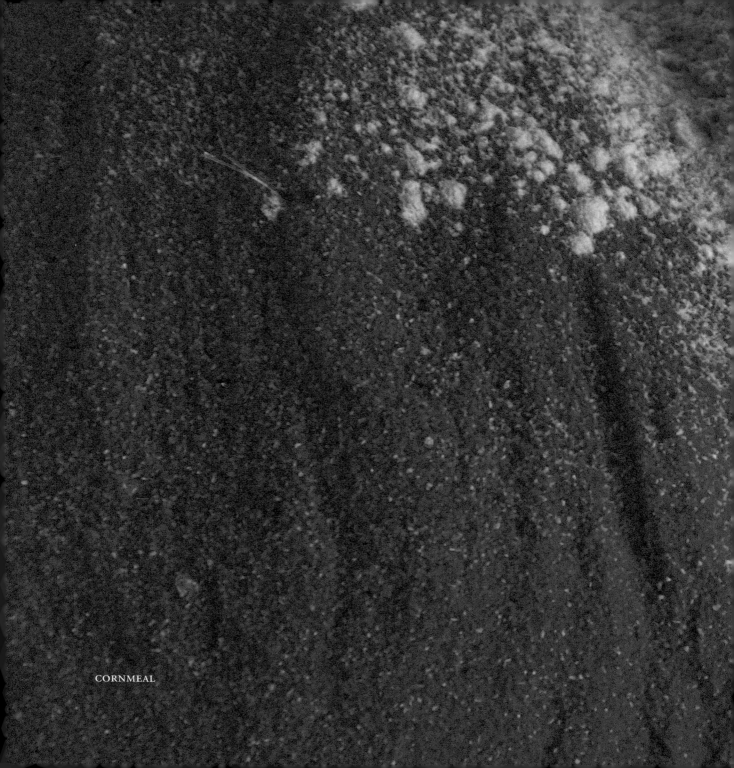

CORNMEAL

Hazelnut Polenta Cake

DAVID MINCEY

YIELD: 1 cake, or 15 individual servings

1½ cups (375 mL) unsalted butter

2 cups (500 mL) sugar

6 eggs

12 egg yolks

1¼ cups (310 mL) coarse cornmeal

1¾ cups (435 mL) all-purpose flour

1 cup (250 mL) hazelnuts, toasted, skinned and finely chopped

1½ tsp (7 mL) baking powder

1 tsp (5 mL) salt

Preheat the oven to 350°F (180°C). In a large mixing bowl, cream butter and sugar together using a mixer with a paddle attachment. Add eggs slowly, mixing well after each addition. In a medium mixing bowl, combine all the dry ingredients, then add to batter one-third at a time. Be careful not to overwork the batter—just mix until there are no longer any dry bits.

Pour the batter into a well-oiled 9 × 13-inch (3.5 L) cake pan or 15 individual ramekins. Bake for 30 minutes, or until cake is well risen and a tester comes out clean.

Chef's tip: This is a recipe we have used for many years at Camille's. If hazelnuts are not available, most other nuts will work. Shredded coconut also makes a tasty substitution.

Prune Plum Clafouti

CHRISTABEL PADMORE

YIELD: 6–8 servings

Preheat the oven to 350°F (180°C). Butter an ovenproof baking dish with a depth of about 1½ inches (4 cm) and set aside.

Halve plums and remove pits. Place in a bowl and sprinkle with kirsch and ⅓ cup (80 mL) of the sugar. Set aside.

In a blender, blend milk, remaining ⅓ cup (80 mL) sugar, eggs, vanilla, salt and flour until fully mixed.

Pour a ¼-inch (6 mm) layer of batter into the prepared baking dish. Place in the oven for about 5 minutes, until a film of batter has set in the bottom of the dish.

Remove from the oven and spread the plums and accumulated liquid over the batter with the skins facing up. Pour the rest of the batter overtop.

Bake on the middle rack of the oven for about 1 hour, until the clafouti has puffed up and browned and a toothpick or knife plunged into its centre comes out clean. Sprinkle with icing sugar before serving.

1 lb (500 g) Italian prune plums, firm and ripe
2 Tbsp (30 mL) kirsch or other liqueur
⅔ cup (160 mL) white sugar, divided
1¼ cup (310 mL) milk
3 eggs
1 Tbsp (15 mL) vanilla extract
⅛ tsp (0.5 mL) salt
½ cup (125 mL) all-purpose flour
icing sugar, for garnishing

Quince Paste

MATT RISSLING AND LIFECYCLES' FRUIT TREE PROJECT

whole quince

organic cane sugar

Preheat the oven to 350°F (180°C). Place quince on baking sheets and roast until skins are loosened. Remove from oven and peel, core and roughly chop.

For every 1 pound (500 g) of cooked quince, measure out ½ pound (250 g) sugar. In a large pot over medium-low heat, bring fruit and sugar to a simmer. Reduce heat and stir often, simmering until fruit begins to gel slightly, about 2–3 hours. Remove from heat and purée with an immersion blender.

Line cake pans with parchment paper and pour a layer of purée 1½ inches (4 cm) deep. Place pans in a very low-temperature oven (ideally 105°F [41°C]) and let dry for 12–24 hours.

Turn quince paste out onto parchment-lined baking sheets, cover loosely and set aside in a dry, cool area. Cure for 2 weeks, flipping every 1–2 days. (If spoilage occurs, trim off spoiled area. To avoid spoilage, keep hands and equipment very clean throughout process.)

After 2 weeks, place quince paste in airtight containers and store at room temperature or place in the freezer for long-term storage.

Social Enterprise and LifeCycles Project Society

By participating in LifeCycles' social enterprise initiatives, volunteers help make value-added products like our infamous quince paste and also enjoy learning new skills while connecting with a network of like-minded people. Our business partners also help create new products for their customers while engaging with LifeCycles' work and raising their company's profile in the community. Customers who buy the resulting products get access to socially conscious and sustainably produced foods while learning about LifeCycles' mission of health and urban sustainability. The profits from this social enterprise go towards supporting the Fruit Tree Project, providing the program with long-term sustainability and assisting with harvesting and redistributing more fruit that might otherwise be wasted. Social entreprise also increases LifeCycles' presence in the community, helping to attract new members and volunteers.

LifeCycles' quince paste is made from quince picked by Fruit Tree Project volunteers from trees located in Greater Victoria. With this particular partnership, volunteers have the opportunity to take the project to the next level by participating in the creation of a value-added product. Thanks to the donation of the Marina Restaurant's kitchen space, as well as some staff time, LifeCycles volunteers get to experience making the product on a commercial scale. After the quince paste is cured, LifeCycles staff wrap it and bring most of it to Ottavio Italian Bakery & Delicatessen where it is sold and redistributed, with the majority of proceeds going back to LifeCycles' Fruit Tree Project.

This endeavour is a unique opportunity: LifeCycles volunteers and the business community get to connect and learn more about each other, fruit that would normally go to waste is used in a beneficial way for the community and it is a great fundraising opportunity for the Fruit Tree Project. The community loves it too. As Chef Matt says, it's where the rubber meets the road.

By supporting socially minded local businesses and providing ethically produced food to community members, social enterprise helps to build up Victoria's social economy, increasing our capacity to live and flourish sustainably as a city.

For more information, see lifecyclesproject.ca.

CHANTERELLES AT THEIR PEAK

FOREST

Drunken Blueberries with Honey Ricotta

JAMES MCCLELLAN

YIELD: 6–8 servings

1 lb (500 g) fresh local blueberries
    (try Silverside Farms)
4 oz (125 mL) Grand Marnier
2 cups (500 mL) ricotta cheese
    (try Paradise Island)
2 oz (60 mL) honey (try Tugwell Creek)
icing sugar and fresh mint
    sprigs, for garnishing

In a medium mixing bowl, pour Grand Marnier over-top blueberries. Cover and set aside for 1 hour. In a small mixing bowl, mix ricotta cheese and honey.

To serve, spoon honey ricotta into bowls or wine glasses and top with blueberries. Garnish with icing sugar and a sprig of fresh mint.

HEIRLOOM SEEDS

CHANTERELLES

Chanterelles on Toast

CHRISTABEL PADMORE

YIELD: 4 servings, as an appetizer

In a sauté pan over medium-high heat, melt 1 tablespoon (30 mL) of butter. Add mushrooms and cook until wilted. Deglaze pan with fortified wine. Add cream, thyme (if using) and simmer until reduced by half and consistency has thickened. Season with salt and pepper, then serve on toasted bread.

2 Tbsp (30 mL) butter, divided

½ lb (250 g) chanterelle mushrooms, cleaned

2 Tbsp (30 mL) fortified wine (sherry, madeira, marsala, etc.)

¾ cup (185 mL) heavy cream

1 tsp (5 mL) fresh thyme (optional)

salt and pepper, to taste

4 slices of white bread (preferably something rich like brioche or challah), toasted

DRAGON TONGUE BEANS

Fiddlehead and Goat Cheese Tortilla

CHRISTABEL PADMORE

YIELD: 4–6 servings

1 lb (500 g) fiddleheads
8 large eggs
salt and pepper, to taste
2 Tbsp (30 mL) whipping cream
2 Tbsp (30 mL) butter
1 lb (500 g) Yukon Gold
    potatoes, boiled and sliced
5 Tbsp (75 mL) goat cheese

Preheat the oven to 350°F (180°C).

Rinse and dry fiddleheads. Using a paring knife, clean off any remaining dirt and trim the stems.

In a large bowl, whisk eggs, adding salt, pepper and cream.

Fill a medium saucepan with water and a pinch of salt. Bring to a boil. Add fiddleheads and blanch for 2 minutes. Remove from water, drain immediately and transfer to a flat surface to cool.

Butter a 10-inch (3 L) baking dish. Arrange slices of potatoes over the bottom of the dish. Sprinkle with salt and pepper, then arrange fiddleheads overtop potatoes and sprinkle with salt and pepper. Dot the fiddleheads with the goat cheese. Pour egg mixture overtop vegetables and cheese. Place in oven and cook for 20–25 minutes, or until set.

Remove from oven and serve.

Foraged Mushroom Tart

PATRICK SIMPSON

YIELD: 4 servings, as an appetizer

Preheat the oven to 350°F (180°C).

Roll out puff pastry to ¼ inch (6 mm) thickness. Poke with a fork. Place on an ungreased baking sheet and parbake for about 10 minutes, removing from the oven before it begins to brown.

In a sauté pan over medium heat, melt butter, then add mushrooms. Sauté mushrooms until tender. Deglaze the pan with sherry. Remove from heat and add goat cheese, thyme, salt and pepper.

Spread mushroom mixture overtop pastry. Return to oven and bake until pastry is golden and cheese begins to bubble. Can be served hot, or cool down for a picnic.

½ lb (250 g) block puff pastry, defrosted

2 Tbsp (30 mL) butter

1 lb (500 g) foraged mushrooms (chanterelles, morels, etc.), cleaned and sliced

½ cup (125 mL) goat cheese

2 Tbsp (30 mL) sherry

1 tsp (5 mL) fresh thyme

salt and pepper, to taste

LOBSTER MUSHROOMS

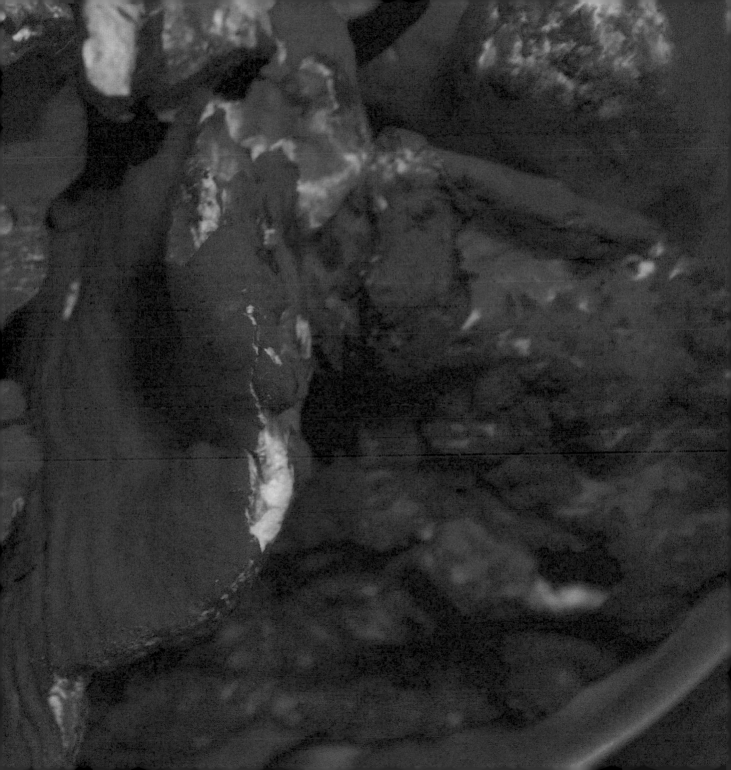

Grand Fir Pavlova with Rosehip Pressed Yogourt and Rhubarb Compote

BILL JONES

YIELD: 8–10 servings

Pavlova

1 tsp (5 mL) pure vanilla extract

1 tsp (5 mL) white vinegar (or ½ tsp [2 mL] cream of tartar)

2 Tbsp (30 mL) Grand Fir needles, finely minced

1½ Tbsp (22.5 mL) cornstarch

1½ cups (375 mL) white sugar

6 egg whites (from large eggs)

pinch of salt

Position a rack in the middle of the oven and preheat the oven to 275°F (140°C). Line a large baking sheet with parchment paper.

In a small cup, combine vanilla, vinegar (if using) and Grand Fir needles. In a small bowl, stir together cornstarch and sugar.

In the large bowl of a heavy-duty mixer fitted with a whisk attachment, whip egg whites, cream of tartar (if using) and salt, starting on low and increasing incrementally to medium speed until soft peaks/trails start to become visible and the egg white bubbles are very small and uniform, approximately 2–3 minutes.

Increase mixer speed to medium-high, slowly and gradually sprinkling in the sugar-cornstarch mixture. A few minutes after these dry ingredients have been added, slowly pour in the vanilla mixture. Gradually increase the speed and whip until meringue is glossy and stiff peaks form when the whisk is lifted, about 4–5 minutes.

Pipe or spoon the meringue into 8–10 large round mounds that are 3 inches (8 cm) wide. With the back of a spoon, create an indentation in the middle of each mound for holding the filling once the meringues are baked.

Place the baking sheet in the oven. Reduce the oven temperature to 250°F (120°C). Bake for 50–60 minutes, or until meringues are crisp, dry to the touch on the outside and white, not tan-coloured or cracked. The interiors should have a marshmallow-like consistency. Check on meringues at least once during baking time. If they appear to be taking on colour or cracking, reduce the temperature by 25 degrees and rotate the pan.

When meringues are done, gently lift off the baking sheet and cool on a wire rack. Meringues will keep in a tightly sealed container at room temperature, or individually wrapped, for up to a week if your house is not humid.

Pressed Yogourt

Line a sieve with two layers of paper towel. Add yogourt and place overtop a bowl. Allow to drain for 1 hour. Transfer yogourt to a container and stir in rosehip preserves. Taste and adjust sweetness, adding more preserves (or honey) if necessary.

Rhubarb Compote

In a saucepan over medium heat, combine all the ingredients and cook until rhubarb begins to give off moisture. Reduce to a simmer and cook until rhubarb is tender but not starting to break down. Remove from heat and allow to cool. Chill for at least 1 hour before using.

To assemble pavlovas, top each meringue with a scoop of yogourt mixture and garnish with a spoonful of rhubarb compote.

Yogourt
4 cups (1 L) yogourt
1 Tbsp (30 mL) rosehip
    preserves (or honey)

Compote
4 cups (1 L) fresh rhubarb, chopped
¼ cup (60 mL) dry white wine
1 cup (250 mL) white sugar
2 Tbsp (30 mL) candied
    ginger, finely chopped

Rabbit Stew with Foraged Mushrooms

PATRICK SIMPSON

YIELD: 6 servings

4 slices bacon, diced

4 lb (1.8 kg) rabbit, cut into 8–10 pieces

salt and ground pepper, to taste

2 Tbsp (30 mL) all-purpose flour

2 Tbsp (30 mL) olive oil

3 garlic cloves, minced

2 cups (500 mL) dry white wine

1½ cups (375 mL) foraged mushrooms
(chanterelles, morels, lobster
mushrooms), sliced

1 bay leaf

½ tsp (2 mL) fresh thyme, chopped

⅓ cup (80 mL) whipping cream

In a heavy pot, like a Dutch oven, sauté the diced bacon until crisp. Remove and set aside. Keep the bacon fat in the pan.

Sprinkle rabbit pieces with salt and pepper and dredge with flour. Add olive oil to the bacon fat in the pot and sauté rabbit pieces over medium heat until they are brown on all sides. Once brown, remove the rabbit from the pot and set aside.

Add garlic to the pot. Over high heat, deglaze the pot with white wine, bring to a boil, then reduce to a simmer. Return the rabbit to the pot and add the mushrooms, bay leaf and thyme. Let simmer for 1 hour over low heat or in the oven at 350°F (180°C). The rabbit is ready when the meat begins to fall from the bone. Add the bacon and the cream. Season with salt and pepper, then cook, uncovered, for 10 minutes. Serve with rice or pasta.

Stinging Nettle and White Bean Soup with Sheep's Sorrel

BROCK WINDSOR

YIELD: 6 servings

Pick stinging nettles carefully while wearing rubber gloves. Blanch nettles in boiling water for 2 minutes, refresh in ice water, wring dry and chop coarsely. Set aside.

In a large pot over medium heat, sauté vegetables and garlic in oil, stirring often. Add beans, herbs, spices and stock and bring to a simmer. Cook until everything is soft. Add nettles and cook for 5 more minutes.

Add the sheep's sorrel and check the seasoning.

15 stinging nettle tops (harvest from February to May)

1 large carrot, coarsely chopped

1 large onion, coarsely chopped

2 celery stalks or root, coarsely chopped

3 cloves garlic, coarsely chopped

2 Tbsp (30 mL) flavourless oil (try grapeseed oil)

½ cup (125 mL) cooked white beans (soak dry beans overnight and then cook until soft)

4 sprigs of fresh thyme

1 bay leaf

6 cups (1.5 L) vegetable stock

25 sheep's sorrel leaves, chopped

sea salt and pepper, to taste

Wilted Lamb's Quarters with Nodding Onion

BROCK WINDSOR

YIELD: 4 servings, as an accompaniment

1 nodding onion, minced
1 Tbsp (15 mL) grapeseed oil
1 Tbsp (15 mL) butter
30 lamb's quarters tops
salt and pepper, to taste
splash of apple cider vinegar

In a saucepan over medium heat, sweat onion in oil and butter until soft but not brown. Add lamb's quarters and cook until the leaves wilt, season with salt, pepper and vinegar and serve immediately.

Chef's tip: Substitute 1 tablespoon (15 mL) of chives or green onion for the nodding onion.

I think the best thing about lamb's quarters, besides being free for the picking, is that they don't taste bitter, astringent or sour, which can be the case with some wild greens. Incredibly healthy, they are also known as goosefoot or pigweed. I like them up to 1 inch (2.5 cm) tall, and they like freshly turned soil, so when weeding your beds, save the lamb's quarters tops—and note that after you cut off the top, shortly the side leaves all have tops of their own. You could add them at the end of almost any savoury recipe, as you would spinach. They are edible raw in salads although they have a white powdery substance on them that makes them more palatable cooked.

ITALIAN SUNFLOWERS

FIELD

Grilled Asparagus Salad with Tarragon Vinaigrette

CHRISTABEL PADMORE

YIELD: 4 servings, as an appetizer

Vinaigrette
1 Tbsp (15 m) fresh tarragon, minced
1 tsp (5 tsp) Dijon mustard
1 tsp (5 mL) honey (5 mL)
2 Tbsp (30 mL) white wine vinegar
4 Tbsp (60 mL) olive oil
salt and pepper, to taste

1 lb (500 g) asparagus

To make dressing, combine all ingredients and whisk until emulsified. Set aside.

Trim and peel asparagus. Grill on the barbecue until al dente (or blanch asparagus in boiling water if grill is not available).

Toss asparagus in dressing and serve immediately, or refrigerate and serve within 4 hours.

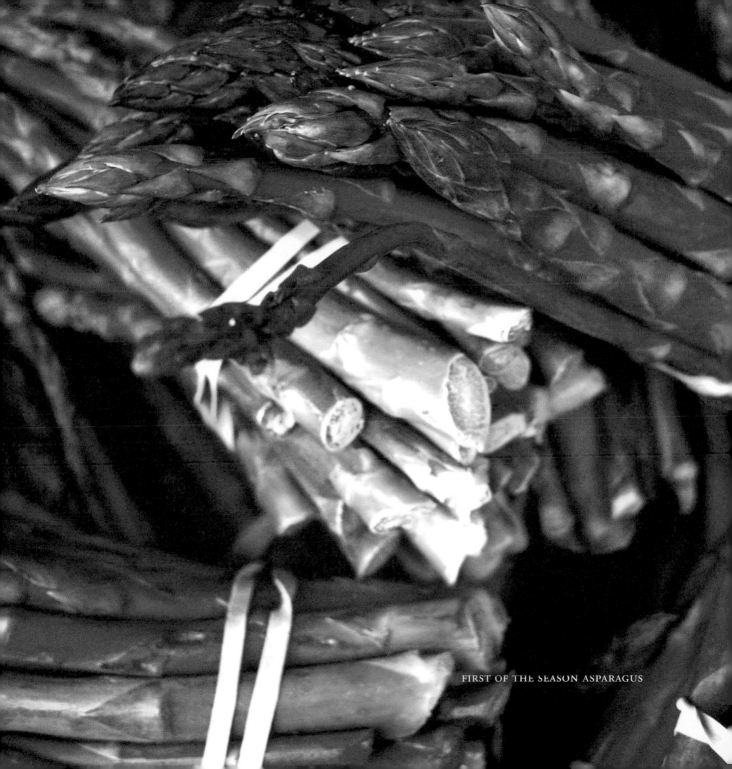

FIRST OF THE SEASON ASPARAGUS

GOLDEN SAANICH BEETS

Organic Beet and Kale Salad with Salt Spring Island Goat Cheese

ASH LENICK

YIELD: 4–6 servings

Place raw beets in a stockpot and fill with enough water to submerge beets. Add 1 cup (250 mL) of the vinegar, ¼ cup (60 mL) of the cane sugar and 4 tablespoons (60 mL) of the salt to the pot. Bring to a boil and cook over medium-high for 40 minutes.

Remove from heat and peel beets with a paring knife. Cut beets into ¼-inch (6 mm) discs and then julienne. Wash kale and remove all stems. Coarsely chop and set aside while you prepare the vinaigrette.

To a blender, add mustard, shallot, garlic and pepper along with remaining vinegar, sugar and salt. Cover and purée on high speed. Once ingredients have been puréed until smooth, slowly add olive oil until it is all incorporated.

To a large mixing bowl, add julienned beets and chopped kale, and mix well with vinaigrette.

Sprinkle goat cheese overtop. Serve and enjoy!

5 lb (2.2 kg) locally grown red beets

1¼ cups (310 mL) white balsamic vinegar, divided

¼ cup plus ¾ Tbsp (71 mL) cane sugar, divided

4 Tbsp plus ½ tsp (62 mL) fine sea salt, divided

2 lb (1 kg) locally grown kale, stems removed

1½ Tbsp (22.5 mL) grainy mustard

1 shallot or small onion, peeled

2 cloves garlic

½ tsp (2 mL) ground white pepper

1 cup (250 mL) pomace olive oil

8 oz (250 g) Salt Spring Island goat cheese, crumbled

Celeriac Remoulade

ANNA HUNT

YIELD: 4–6 servings

2 egg yolks
1 tsp (6 mL) salt
2 Tbsp (30 mL) grainy mustard
8 gherkins
⅓ cup (80 mL) capers
2 cloves garlic
juice of 1 lemon
⅓ cup plus 2 Tbsp (110 mL) canola oil
2 medium-sized celeriac
2 Tbsp (30 mL) chopped
    fresh parsley or chives

In a food processor, combine first 7 ingredients.

Process and begin adding the oil in a very slow gentle stream. Don't rush this step, take your time to ensure the remoulade emulsifies properly. You should end up with a mayo-like consistency. Set the remoulade aside.

Using a sharp knife, trim the skin off the celeriac. Be sure to remove the small hairs that get trapped in the creases. Julienne the root by cutting it into matchsticks with a knife or by using a mandolin if you have one.

Mix the remoulade into celeriac until well coated and then add parsley or chives.

Serve chilled with the protein of your choice.

Can be made in advance and will keep for 3–4 days in the refrigerator.

Fresh Corn Salad

HEIDI FINK

YIELD: 8 servings

Bring a large pot of salted water to a boil. Drop in corn, return to a boil and cook for 1–2 minutes. Use tongs to remove corn and let them cool until you can touch them comfortably.

Meanwhile, mix dressing ingredients together in a small bowl or jar, shaking the jar or mixing with a whisk, until all ingredients are well blended.

In a medium-large bowl, combine half of the dressing with the green onions.

Using a sharp knife, cut all the kernels of corn off the cooked cobs directly into the bowl containing the dressing and the onions. Once the kernels have been removed, use the back of the knife to scrape along the cobs and push all of the corn germ into the bowl.

Stir in the remaining dressing, tomatoes and cilantro. Mix well. Taste and add more salt and/or additional lime juice if you like.

Decorate the top with avocado slices (if using) and serve.

Salad

12 cobs of local fresh sweet corn, shucked

3–4 green onions, sliced

3 large tomatoes, seeded and chopped

1 small bunch cilantro, roughly chopped

1 large ripe avocado, peeled, pitted and thinly sliced (optional)

Dressing

½ cup (125 mL) extra-virgin olive oil

finely minced zest from ½ a lime

¼ cup (60 mL) freshly squeezed lime juice (from 2 fresh limes)

½ tsp (2 mL) salt, or more to taste

1 tsp (5 mL) honey or brown sugar

1 clove garlic, minced or pressed

Crispy Zucchini with Spaghetti

CHRISTABEL PADMORE

YIELD: 4–6 servings

1 Tbsp (15 mL) butter

½ cup (125 mL) olive oil, divided

2 lb (1 kg) zucchini (smaller is better), trimmed and sliced into ¼-inch (6 mm) slices

1 lb (500 g) dry spaghetti

2 Tbsp (30 mL) fresh oregano, minced

1 tsp (5 mL) dry red chili flakes

salt and pepper, to taste

6 Tbsp (90 mL) grated Parmesan cheese, for garnishing

Bring a large pot of salted water to a boil.

Meanwhile, in a large sauté pan, heat butter and 2 tablespoons (60 mL) of the olive oil just until oil begins to smoke. Add zucchini in batches (do not overcrowd the pan). Sauté until brown and crispy. Sprinkle with salt and pepper and set aside.

Cook pasta in the boiling water until al dente.

Drain pasta and return to pot.

Add zucchini, oregano, chili flakes, remaining olive oil, salt and pepper.

Toss and serve immediately, garnished with Parmesan cheese.

ZUCCHINI BLOSSOMS READY FOR STUFFING

Eggplant Pakoras

HEIDI FINK

YIELD: 30 pakoras

Pakoras

1 tsp (5 mL) cumin seeds

1 Tbsp (15 mL) coriander seeds

¼ tsp (1 mL) ajwain seeds (carom)

¼ tsp (1 mL) fennel seeds

½ cup (125 mL) chickpea flour (besan)

¾ tsp (4 mL) salt

¼ tsp (1 mL) baking powder

¼ tsp (1 mL) cayenne

1 tsp (5 mL) finely grated fresh ginger

3 cloves garlic, peeled and sliced thin

1 jalapeno, seeded and sliced

¼ cup (60 mL) chopped cilantro

3–5 small eggplants, sliced ¼ inch
    (6 mm) thick (halve first if large)

2 cups (500 mL) vegetable oil, for frying

Warm a small, dry frying pan over medium heat. When hot, add cumin seeds, coriander seeds, ajwain seeds and fennel seeds. Toast, stirring frequently, until seeds turn a shade darker and give off a nutty fragrance. Be careful not to burn seeds; turn down the heat if necessary.

Transfer toasted seeds to a bowl and let cool. When cool, grind seeds to a powder in a clean coffee grinder or dedicated spice grinder.

In a large bowl, combine ground spices with chickpea flour, salt, baking powder and cayenne. Use a whisk to mix everything well.

Add ⅓ cup (80 mL) water, whisking until a smooth batter forms.

Add ginger, garlic, jalapeno and cilantro, and stir well. Add eggplant.

Use a big spoon to stir everything together, mixing until eggplant pieces are all evenly coated with batter. Add a little extra water, if necessary, to make the batter thin enough to coat all the vegetables.

Heat the oil in a large cast iron pan or in a deep fryer.

Line a large tray with several layers of paper towels or brown paper. The oil is at the right temperature when a piece of battered eggplant sizzles immediately when dropped into the oil, but doesn't burn.

Drop spoonfuls of pakora mixture into the hot oil (a couple of eggplant slices per spoonful).

Pakoras will take about 7–8 minutes to cook. Turn them several times during cooking, so they brown evenly on all sides. Pakoras should be golden brown, but not burnt. Adjust the heat as necessary while cooking.

When ready, remove pakoras with a slotted spoon and place them on the paper-towel-lined tray to drain. Repeat with remaining batter.

Meanwhile, make the dipping sauce. Mix vinegar, sugar and salt together in a medium bowl, and allow to dissolve.

Finely mince herbs and green onions and add to the vinegar mixture, stirring to mix well.

Pakoras may be served hot or at room temperature. They can be stored in the fridge and reheated in a 350°F (180°C) oven for 10 minutes before serving.

Serve with dipping sauce or tamarind chutney.

Quick Dipping Sauce

6 Tbsp (90 mL) rice wine vinegar

2–3 Tbsp (30–90 mL) white or light brown sugar

pinch of salt

1 cup (250 mL) packed cilantro and/or mint leaves

3 green onions

HEIRLOOM EGGPLANT

Golden Harvest Soup

HEIDI FINK

YIELD: 6–8 servings

Soup

3 Tbsp (45 mL) butter

1½ medium yellow onions, diced

1 tsp (5 mL) freshly grated ginger (optional)

2 bay leaves

6 cups (1.5 L) stock or water

1 tsp (5 mL) salt, or more to taste

2 lb (1 kg) acorn or butternut squash
    (5–6 cups [1.25–1.5 L]
    peeled and chopped)

4 large ripe pears (about 4–5 cups
    [1–1.25 L] peeled and chopped)

Prepare soup by warming a heavy soup pot over medium-high heat. Add butter and heat until melted and frothy. Add onions and stir. Sauté, stirring frequently, until onions are translucent and cooked through.

Turn heat down, and continue to cook until onions are deep gold and caramelized. This will take over 20 minutes.

When onions are ready, stir in ginger (if using) and bay leaves and sauté until fragrant, a few seconds.

Add stock or water, salt and chopped squash. Bring to a boil, simmer for a few minutes, then add chopped pears and bring to a boil again.

Reduce heat to low, cover, and simmer until everything is fall-apart tender, about 15–20 minutes.

Remove bay leaves. Purée the soup using a hand-held immersion blender, or in batches in a counter-top blender.

Return soup to pot if using a counter-top blender, and taste to see if it needs more salt.

Prepare garnish by placing chopped candied ginger and about ½ cup (125 mL) of the cream in the bowl of a food processor. Purée, stopping to scrape down the sides as necessary, until the mixture is as smooth as possible.

Scrape ginger crème into a bowl and stir in remaining cream until garnish reaches desired consistency. If you are going to serve the crème in a dollop, add less than ½ cup (125 mL) more cream. If you are going to put the crème into a squirt bottle to make swirly designs in the soup, add a full cup (250 mL) extra cream to make it thin enough to pour.

To serve, ladle soup into bowls and garnish with a dollop or swirl of ginger crème. Serve immediately.

Sweet Ginger Crème Garnish
½ cup (125 mL) candied ginger, chopped
1–1½ cups (250–375 mL)
    heavy cream, divided

REAL CARROTS

Gorditas with Potato and Chorizo

CHRISTABEL PADMORE

YIELD: 16 gorditas

Prepare the dough by combining dry ingredients in a large bowl. Mix, then add oil and combine with your fingers. Make a well in the centre and slowly add 1 cup (250 mL) water. Form dough into a ball and knead for about 5 minutes. Let the dough rest for 10 minutes and prepare the filling.

Warm a sauté pan to medium-high. Add vegetable oil and add onions and garlic when it's hot. When onions and garlic have become translucent, add sausage, pepper and cumin. Sauté until sausage is a little bit crispy. Add potatoes and stir. Remove from the heat and set aside.

To assemble gorditas, cut the dough into approximately 16 even pieces. Roll the pieces out into rounds. Heat about ½ inch (1 cm) of oil in a frying pan. When it's hot, fry the rounds, allowing them to puff up. Drain on paper towels.

Stuff gorditas with potato filling and serve hot with chili sauce and sour cream if you wish.

Dough

3 cups (750 mL) masa harina (or substitute 2 cups [500 mL] all-purpose flour and 1 cup [250 mL]) cornmeal)

½ tsp (2 mL) baking soda

1 tsp (5 mL) salt

1 Tbsp (15 mL) vegetable oil

Filling

1 Tbsp (15 mL) vegetable oil

½ cup (125 mL) onions, chopped

2 cloves garlic, minced

1½ cups (375 mL) chorizo sausage, chopped ¼ inch (6 mm) thick

1 tsp (5 mL) black pepper

1 Tbsp (15 mL) cumin seeds

1½ cups (375 mL) potatoes, boiled and chopped (peel first if desired)

oil, for frying

Gorditas are named after a friendly term to describe roly-poly people.

Roasted Green Bean Crostini

HEIDI FINK

YIELD: 20–24 crostini

1½ lb (750 g) fresh green beans

4 Tbsp (60 mL) extra-virgin
olive oil, divided

1 tsp (5 mL) salt, divided

2 cloves garlic, minced or pressed

3–4 small red ripe tomatoes, minced
(try Sun Wing Tomatoes for
excellent spring tomatoes)

1 tsp (5 mL) balsamic vinegar,
preferably Venturi-Schulze

¼ tsp (1 mL) freshly ground black pepper

¼ cup (60 mL) minced fresh basil or
parsley (or use a mixture of both)

1 good-quality baguette, sliced

extra-virgin olive oil, for brushing

Tomme D'Or or Parmigiano
cheese, for topping

Preheat the oven to 400°F (200°C).

Prepare green beans by topping and tailing each bean. If using for a side vegetable, leave them long. If using them for a crostini topping, cut into small pieces, less than ½ inch (1 cm) long. Toss prepared green beans with 1 tablespoon (15 mL) of the olive oil and ½ teaspoon (2.5 mL) of the salt, coating evenly with oil and salt. Spread beans out in a thin, even layer on a parchment-lined tray. Roast in the oven for about 20–30 minutes if long, or 10–15 minutes if short, stirring once during the cooking time, until beans are spotted brown and tender.

Meanwhile, mix together in a large bowl the remaining olive oil, garlic, tomatoes, balsamic vinegar, salt, pepper and herbs.

When green beans are done, remove them from the oven and immediately dump them into the bowl with the tomato mixture. Mix well to coat beans evenly with the marinade. Let cool slightly and serve, or cool the beans to room temperature and serve as a salad or a topping for crostini. Reduce oven temperature to 350°F (180°C).

Prepare crostini by placing baguette slices flat on a cookie sheet. Brush each slice with olive oil. Place tray in the oven and bake for about 10 minutes. Remove from the oven and let baguette pieces cool to room temperature. Cover each crostini with a tablespoon or two (15–30 mL) of the bean mixture, including some juice. Top with a few shavings of cheese. Serve at room temperature, or reheat briefly in a 350°F (180°C) oven, until cheese is just melted. Serve immediately.

Roasting is an unusual and delicious way of cooking green beans. The high, dry heat of the oven intensifies their flavours and caramelizes the natural sugars in this summer vegetable. Tossed with a delicious marinade, roasted green beans can be used as a side vegetable, a warm or cold salad, or used as a topping for bruschetta or crostini—a fantastic appetizer. The beauty of crostini is that all the individual components (crostini bread, different toppings, shaved cheese) can be prepared ahead of time and the crostini assembled just before serving. Crostini can be served at room temperature, or heated for a few minutes in a 350°F (180°C) oven.

CHANTERELLE PIZZA

Kale Caesar

ANNA HUNT

YIELD: 6 servings

Dressing
½ of a 2-oz (56 g) can anchovies
1 tsp (5 mL) Dijon mustard
1 egg
2 dashes Worcestershire sauce
juice of ½ a lemon
1 clove garlic
1 tsp (5 mL) salt
1 cup (250 mL) vegetable oil

Croutons
2 cups (500 mL) torn sourdough bread
3 Tbsp (45 mL) olive oil
1 Tbsp (15 mL) minced garlic
pinch of fresh stemmed thyme leaves
pinch of salt
cracked pepper, to taste

Salad
2 bunches of Red Russian kale
    (or substitute Lacinato kale)
½ cup (125 mL) cooked chopped bacon
pinch of salt
1 cup (250 mL) shaved Parmigiano-
    Reggiano cheese
6 marinated white anchovies
    (or more, depending on your taste)

Preheat the oven to 350°F (180°C).

Place all dressing ingredients except the oil in the bowl of a food processor. With the motor running, very slowly add oil to form a mayo-like dressing. Set aside and prepare the croutons and salad.

Toss together crouton ingredients in a bowl. Place on an ungreased baking sheet and toast in the hot oven for 20 minutes, or until golden brown and crispy.

Wash and stem kale, spinning or patting until very dry. Tear or chop kale into large but manageable pieces.

In a large bowl, mix together kale, bacon, croutons and desired amount of dressing with a pinch more salt. Plate individual salads, or serve in a serving bowl, and garnish with Parmigiano-Reggiano and anchovies.

SAANICH LETTUCE

Kale and Bacon Pie

ANNA HUNT

YIELD: 6–8 servings

In a bowl, combine flour and salt. Using a pastry cutter, cut in butter until it is the size of peas. Add water and bring dough together with your hands to form a disc. Wrap dough in plastic and allow to rest for a minimum of 4 hours, but preferably overnight (don't worry that it doesn't resemble dough yet—the rolling and resting will look after that).

Preheat the oven to 350°F (180°C). Roll the chilled dough out on a well-floured counter, being sure to rotate it every once in a while to make sure it isn't sticking. Gently lay dough over an 8-inch (20 cm) pie plate, pushing it into the corners but leaving the overhang. Lay some parchment paper or foil over crust and fill it with dry beans.

Place crust on a baking sheet and bake for approximately 30 minutes, or until the edges are beginning to look cooked. Remove beans and parchment or foil and allow crust to bake for another 10 minutes. Remove from the oven and allow to cool. Once cool, use a paring knife to trim off the excess crust from the pan.

Continued on page 104

Dough

1½ cups (375 mL) all-purpose flour

1 tsp (5 mL) salt

½ cup plus 1 Tbsp (140 mL) cold, cubed butter

⅓ cup (80 mL) cold water

Filling

2 bunches of kale

6 slices bacon, chopped

3 shallots, peeled and thinly sliced

2 eggs

1 cup (250 mL) heavy cream

½ cup (125 mL) grated Natural Pastures aged farmhouse cheddar

¾ tsp salt (4 mL)

cracked pepper, to taste

Continued from page 103

While the crust is baking, prepare the filling. Bring a large pot of water to a boil and cook kale for 2 minutes, then strain and cool with cold water. Set aside.

In a frying pan over medium-low heat, render fat from bacon. Add shallots and sweat in bacon fat until they are translucent, about 10 minutes.

While shallots are cooking, squeeze water from kale and give it a rough chop. In a medium bowl, whisk together eggs, cream, cheese, salt and pepper. Set aside.

Add kale to bacon and shallots and combine well. Fill pie crust with kale mixture and pour egg mixture overtop. Return now-filled crust to the oven and bake for 45 minutes, or until the pie looks slightly puffy and the egg in the centre is cooked.

CHIVE BLOSSOMS

Lemon Rosemary Zucchini Bread

GARRETT SCHACK

YIELD: 2 loaves

3 cups (750 mL) all-purpose flour

2 tsp (10 mL) baking soda

½ tsp (2 mL) baking powder

½ tsp (2 mL) salt (omit if
    using salted butter)

2 Tbsp (30 mL) minced fresh rosemary

2 eggs

1¼ cups (310 mL) white sugar

½ cup (125 mL) melted unsalted butter

¼ cup (60 mL) olive oil

1 Tbsp (15 mL) lemon zest

3 cups (750 mL) grated zucchini
    (about 1 lb [500 g])

Preheat the oven to 350°F (180°C) and prepare two 4 × 9-inch (10 × 23 cm) loaf pans, either coating them with butter or baking spray. Set aside.

In a large bowl, whisk together flour, baking soda, baking powder, salt, and rosemary. Set aside.

Beat eggs in a mixer (or by hand) until frothy. Beat in sugar. Beat in melted butter and olive oil. Stir in lemon zest and grated zucchini.

Add the dry ingredients to the wet, a third at a time, stirring after each incorporation, then divide batter/dough between two loaf pans.

Bake in the preheated oven for 45–50 minutes. Test loaves after 40 minutes. If you gently press down on the surface, it should bounce back, and a bamboo skewer inserted into the centre should come out clean.

Remove loaves from the oven. Let cool for a few minutes and then remove from their pans to cool on a rack.

Lemon Risotto with Asparagus

PAUL STEWART

YIELD: 6 servings

Trim off tough ends of asparagus, about an inch (2.5 cm), leaving tips and tender parts of the stalks.

Boil a small pot of salted water, then add asparagus and blanch for only 1 minute, refreshing in cold water. Chop asparagus if desired or leave them whole.

In a medium saucepan, heat butter, then add onions and cook until translucent and soft, about 5 minutes. Add rice and cook until grains start to crack and smell nutty, about 3 minutes.

Add 2 cups (500 mL) of the hot stock, stirring constantly, and lemon zest. As rice absorbs the stock, add one ladleful more at a time, making sure to keep stirring, until rice is slightly al dente, not mushy.

Once rice is cooked, add asparagus and cheese.

Season with salt and pepper, lemon juice and thyme.

1 lb (500 g) fresh asparagus
4 Tbsp (60 mL) butter
1 cup (250 mL) finely chopped white onion
2½ cups (625 mL) Arborio rice
6–7 cups (1.5–1.75 L) vegetable
    or chicken stock, heated, divided
zest of ½ a lemon
¼ cup (60 mL) freshly
    grated Parmesan cheese
salt and pepper, to taste
juice of 1 lemon
2 sprigs chopped fresh thyme, leaves only

Pickled Beets

JAMES MCCLELLAN

YIELD: 6 servings, as part of an antipasto

In a large stockpot, cover beets with 4 cups (1 L) water and bring to a boil, then simmer until fork-tender, about 1.5 hours. Cool and then rub off skins.

In another medium or large pot, place all other ingredients and bring to a boil. Add beets and then let cool.

Beets are best stored in a covered container and refrigerated for at least for 3 days before using. If canned, pickled beets will last up to 1 year if stored in a cool, dry place.

1 lb (500 g) Makaria Farm
    or other local beets
2 cups (500 mL) white vinegar
2 oz (60 g) pickling spice
1 cinnamon stick
1 Tbsp (15 mL) horseradish

Rhubarb Pudding Cake

PATRICK SIMPSON

YIELD: 1 cake

4 cups (1 L) fresh rhubarb, chopped
1½ cups (375 mL) sugar, divided
¼ cup (60 mL) unsalted butter
1 egg
½ tsp (2 mL) vanilla extract
1 cup (250 mL) all-purpose flour
2 tsp (10 mL) baking powder
¼ tsp (1 mL) salt
½ cup (125 mL) milk

Preheat the oven to 350°F (180°C) and grease a 9-inch (23 cm) square pan.

In a large saucepan, combine rhubarb with 1 cup (250 mL) of the sugar and cook for 15 minutes over medium heat. Set aside.

In a mixing bowl, cream remaining sugar with butter until fluffy, then add egg and vanilla.

In a separate bowl, combine flour, baking powder and salt.

Add dry ingredients to butter mixture, alternating with milk.

Pour cake batter into prepared pan. Spread rhubarb mixture on top of the cake batter.

Place in the oven and bake for 35–40 minutes. Check doneness with a toothpick. Cool and serve.

Chef's tip: Garnish with cream whipped with maple syrup for a special treat.

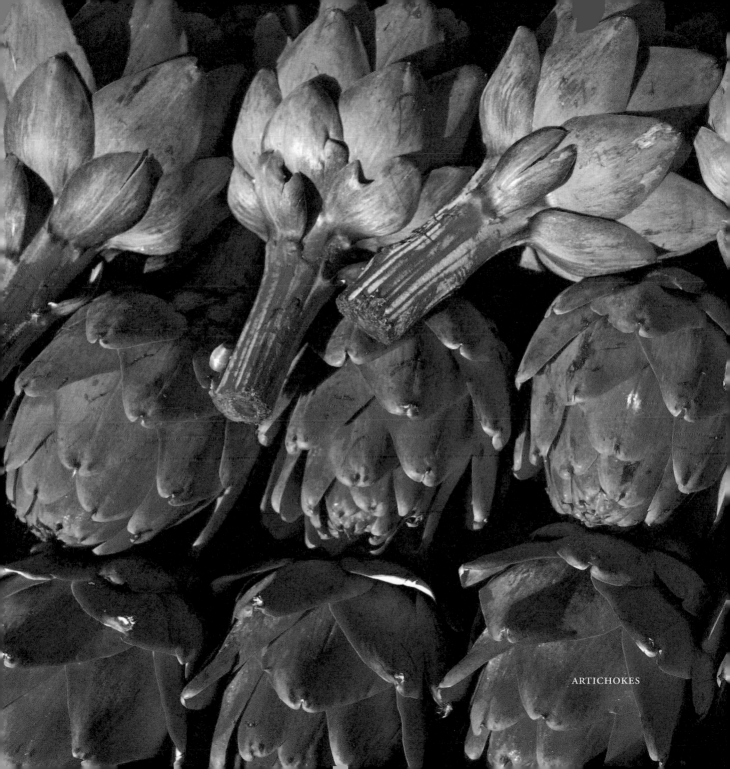

ARTICHOKES

Spinach Salad with Bacon and Citrus Vinaigrette

CHRISTABEL PADMORE

YIELD: 2–4 servings

Vinaigrette

3 rashers lean side bacon, cut into lardons

juice of 1 orange

1 Tbsp (15 mL) shallot, minced

1 tsp (5 mL) honey

1 Tbsp (15 mL) rice wine vinegar, or
    another mild vinegar

1–2 tsp (5–10 mL) olive oil (for balance
    and a bit of flavour), depending
    on the leanness of the bacon

salt and pepper, to taste

Salad

1 bunch baby spinach (preferably local),
    cleaned and trimmed

3–4 small mushrooms, brushed
    clean and sliced

1 Tbsp (15 mL) red or sweet
    onion, very thinly sliced

½ cup (125 mL) Gruyère or
    Emmental cheese, grated

1 hard-boiled free run egg, halved

Add bacon to a hot pan, reducing the temperature to avoid smoking and ensure even cooking. Render fat from bacon and carefully cook bacon until evenly crispy. Leaving bacon and fat in the pan, reduce heat to low. Add orange juice and shallot and allow to reduce by about a quarter.

Add honey, vinegar, olive oil, salt and pepper. Mix and turn off the heat until ready to serve.

To assemble salad, place spinach, mushrooms and onion in a medium-sized bowl. Toss with vinaigrette, then arrange on a platter and garnish with cheese and egg.

Tomatillo Salsa

HEIDI FINK

YIELD: 2 cups (500 mL)

Remove and discard papery husks from tomatillos. Wash tomatillos well and place in a small pot with enough fresh water to just cover them. Bring to a boil, reduce heat and simmer until tomatillos are tender, about 10 minutes.

Drain tomatillos, reserving cooking liquid, and set them and their liquid aside to cool.

Place onion, garlic, cilantro, salt and chilies in the bowl of a food processor or blender. Add ½ cup (125 mL) of cooled tomatillo cooking liquid. Blend until very finely chopped.

Add cooked tomatillos and pulse to make a coarse purée. Pour into a bowl. Taste salsa for salt. Use a little more of the cooking liquid to thin the salsa if necessary.

Serve with tortilla chips or in taco shells.

Chef's tip: To choose tomatillos, look for firm fruit with a dry husk. Tomatillos should not be soft and mushy. The colour of a tomatillo can range from bright apple green to pale yellow. Any colour within that range is fine, although the greener ones are less ripe and therefore less prone to spoiling. Local tomatillos are usually small, only slightly bigger than cherry tomatoes, and often have a dark purple tinge to the husks or fruit.

12 oz (350 g) fresh tomatillos (about 8–12 tomatillos)

½ white or yellow onion, diced

2 cloves garlic

¼ cup (60 mL) minced fresh cilantro

½ tsp (2 mL) salt

1–2 jalapenos or other chilies, chopped (use more if you like it spicy)

Tomatillos are not small green tomatoes. Although in the same family as tomatoes, tomatillos are more closely related to the ground cherry and cape gooseberry. They grow very well in our southern Vancouver Island climate.

BACKYARD CHERRY TOMATOES

Tomato Gazpacho

MATT RISSLING

YIELD: 4–6 servings

In a blender, purée first 5 ingredients well, then strain.

Adjust gazpacho for sweetness with honey, acidity with lemon juice or vinegar, and seasoning with salt and pepper.

Chill and then serve.

3 lb (1.5 kg) ripe tomatoes
1 lb (500 g) long English cucumber
3 shallots, diced
½ cup (125 mL) red wine vinegar
½ cup (125 mL) fresh basil
honey, to taste
lemon juice or vinegar, to taste
salt and pepper, to taste

CHERRY TOMATOES ON THE VINE

FARM

Bison Bulgogi and Butter Lettuce Wraps

CHRISTABEL PADMORE

YIELD: 4–6 servings

Marinade

3 large garlic cloves, minced

3 Tbsp (45 mL) soy sauce

3 green onions, minced

2 Tbsp (30 mL) pear juice (or substitute apple juice)

1 Tbsp (15 mL) honey

1 Tbsp (15 mL) Japanese rice wine (mirin)

1 Tbsp (15 mL) sesame oil

1 tsp (5 mL) ground black pepper

Bulgogi

2 lb (1 kg) bison ribeye

1 head butter lettuce

1.5 cups (375 mL) cooked short grain rice (preferably sticky rice)

Korean spicy bean paste (*Gochijang*) (optional)

kimchi (optional)

Prepare marinade by combining all ingredients together. Slice bison in thin strips and skewer with bamboo skewers. Pour marinade into a large glass dish, add bison skewers, cover and marinate overnight.

Preheat grill to medium. Cook rice in a pot or rice cooker with 3 cups (750 mL) water. Clean and separate lettuce.

Grill bison skewers to desired doneness and serve immediately. To serve, wrap bison in a lettuce leaf with some rice, spicy bean paste and kimchi.

ROWS OF BUTTER LETTUCE

Braised Pork Cheeks with Potato Gnocchi

CORY PELAN

YIELD: 8 servings

Prepare stock by adding all ingredients to a medium-sized pan. Bring to a simmer and cook for 4 hours covered tightly, then strain. Cool stock, then store in fridge until ready to use. Skim off fat before using.

Preheat the oven to 350°F (180°C).

Mix flour with salt and pepper in a medium-sized bowl. Pat dry pork cheeks with paper towels, then dredge in seasoned flour.

Fill a large, deep frying pan with enough oil to cover the meat, then heat oil until almost smoking. Add cheeks and sear until golden brown on both sides. Work in batches to avoid crowding the pan and cooling the oil down. Transfer cheeks to a side plate and drain excess oil from the pan. Deglaze pan by adding half of the prepared stock, being sure to scrape up any of the brown bits on the bottom of the pan.

Add remaining stock and seared cheeks to pan and braise in preheated oven for 2.5 hours. Remove cheeks from pan and heat braising liquid on stovetop over medium heat until reduced by three-quarters.

Continued on page 124

Stock

3 garlic cloves, crushed
1 bottle (750 mL) dry red wine
2 yellow onions, quartered
1 cup (250 mL) large dice carrots
1 cup (250 mL) large dice celery
1 cup (250 mL) water
1 sprig fresh thyme
1 bay leaf
¼ cup (60 mL) balsamic vinegar
½ tsp (2 mL) whole black pepper
1 pork trotter or hock

Pork Cheeks

1 cup (250 mL) all-purpose flour
salt, to taste
½ tsp (2 mL) ground pepper
10 fresh pork cheeks
olive oil, for frying

Gnocchi

2.2 lb (1 kg) Russet potatoes, unpeeled

¾ cup (185 mL) all-purpose flour, divided

1½ Tbsp (22.5 mL) Parmigiano-Reggiano cheese

½ tsp (2 mL) salt

1 egg yolk

When cooked properly, pork cheeks can be an absolutely ethereal eating experience. They are the epitome of the tough under-utilized cut of meat that when prepared slowly and with care can yield truly amazing results. Serve these cheeks on pasta, rice or mashed potatoes, although my favourite way to serve them is on freshly prepared homemade gnocchi with a good amount of grated Parmigiano-Reggiano.

Continued from page 123

Season with salt to taste and return cheeks to pan to heat through. Serve with freshly made gnocchi and Parmigiano-Reggiano cheese.

Potato Gnocchi

In a large pot, cover potatoes with cold water and bring to simmer, cooking until potatoes are tender enough to pierce easily with a fork but not falling apart. Immediately drain and remove skins while still hot.

Pass potatoes through a potato ricer into a large bowl. Add three-quarters of the flour, all of the cheese, the salt and the egg yolk. Mix with your hands until smooth, adding more flour if necessary to create a dough that is not sticky but soft and velvety. (You may need more flour than the recipe calls for depending on the relative humidity and moisture content of the potatoes.)

Roll dough into ½ inch (1 cm) thick ropes and cut into ⅔ inch (1.5 cm) lengths. Roll across a gnocchi board or use a fork to create ridges. Store on a well-floured sheet pan in the fridge or freezer until ready to cook.

To cook, add gnocchi to a large pot of boiling water. They are done when they float to the surface. Serve with pork cheeks braised in red wine and balsamic vinegar. Top with freshly grated Parmigiano-Reggiano cheese.

Comox Brie Quiche with Butternut Squash

ALESHA DAVIES

YIELD: 8-inch (20 cm) pie

1 Tbsp (15 mL) organic olive oil

1 medium onion, chopped

1 garlic clove, minced

½ cup (125 mL) diced butternut squash

1 medium-sized portabella mushroom, chopped

4 organic local farm eggs

¼ cup (60 mL) milk

1 tsp (5 mL) chopped fresh rosemary

1 tsp (5 mL) chopped fresh parsley

salt and pepper, to taste

1 dash hot sauce (any kind will do)

1 homemade (p. 103) or storebought pie crust

1 round Comox Brie cheese (or another type of soft ripened Brie)

Preheat the oven to 375°F (190°C).

In a frying pan over medium heat, add olive oil and sauté onion for 2 minutes. Add garlic and sauté for 2 minutes more.

Add diced squash and sauté for 3 minutes more. Add mushrooms and continue to sauté until onions, squash and mushrooms have all softened but are not mushy.

In a medium-sized bowl, mix together eggs, milk, rosemary, parsley, salt and pepper, and hot sauce. Whisk until well combined; mixture should be bubbly around the edges.

Add the sautéed vegetables to the egg mixture and stir. Pour mixture into prepared pie crust.

Slice Brie into long strips. Lay strips overtop quiche mixture from the middle fanning outwards. Sprinkle with pepper and place in preheated oven for 30–40 minutes.

When gently wiggled, quiche should be fully set (no jiggle) and lightly browned.

Comox Camembert, Blackberry and Walnut Phyllo Bundle

ASH LENICK

YIELD: 2 servings

Preheat the oven to 350°F (180°C).

Coarsely chop berries, then set aside.

Brush both sheets of phyllo pastry with melted butter and fold each piece in half widthwise. Brush top side of one folded phyllo sheet with butter and join the other piece of folded phyllo to it so it resembles a plus-sign shape.

Place cheese in the centre of the plus sign, then spoon berries and walnuts overtop. Carefully join all points of the phyllo together, so it resembles a candy in a wrapper. Place on a baking tray on the middle shelf of the oven for 6–8 minutes, or until phyllo is golden brown. Serve and enjoy!

2 Tbsp (30 mL) seasonal berries (try blackberries or blueberries)

2 sheets phyllo pastry

2 Tbsp (30 mL) melted butter

2-inch (5 cm) cube Comox Camembert cheese

1.5 Tbsp (22.5 mL) chopped walnuts

ORGANIC GARLIC SCAPES

Cheese and Honey Mead Fondue

DWANE MACISAAC

YIELD: 6 servings

1 garlic clove, halved crosswise

1½ cups (375 mL) honey mead

1 Tbsp (15 mL) cornstarch

2 tsp (10 mL) kirsch

2 cups (500 mL) coarsely
    grated Emmental cheese

2 cups (500 mL) coarsely
    grated Gruyère cheese

cubes of artisan bread, for serving

Rub the inside of a heavy-bottomed 4-quart (4 L) pot with cut sides of garlic, then discard garlic. Add mead to pot and bring just to a simmer over moderate heat.

In a cup, stir together cornstarch and kirsch. Set aside.

Gradually add cheesees to pot and cook. Stir constantly in a zigzag pattern (not a circular motion) to prevent cheese from balling up, until cheese is melted and creamy. Do not let boil.

Stir cornstarch mixture again and stir into fondue. Bring fondue to a simmer and cook, stirring, until thickened, about 5–8 minutes.

Transfer to a fondue pot set over a low to medium flame and serve with artisan breads for dipping.

TENDER CHARD

Chicken Confit with Creamed Corn

JONATHAN PULKNER

YIELD: 6 servings, as a main course

Using a mortar and pestle, crush together garlic, thyme, bay leaves and salt. Rub chicken legs with the salt mixture, then lay in a single layer in a shallow baking dish, pressing them down gently. Refrigerate overnight.

Preheat the oven to 250°F (120°C).

In a heavy ovenproof pot, melt duck fat. Rinse salt mixture off chicken legs and pat dry. Gently place legs into the melted fat and bring to a gentle simmer. Place the pot in the oven and cook for 2 hours, or until joints of legs are loose and meat is ready to fall off the bone. Allow to cool.

Place legs in a storage crock with a tight-fitting lid and add enough of the fat to cover them completely. The confit is now preserved and ready to store in the fridge for later use.

To serve confit, preheat the oven to 375°F (190°C). Heat a cast iron pan and add a small amount of fat from the confit and a small knob of butter. Add chicken skin side down and put in the oven for 10–15 minutes, or until heated through and skin is crispy.

Continued on page 134

Confit
3 cloves garlic
fresh thyme sprigs
2 bay leaves
¼ cup (60 mL) coarse sea salt
6 free-range chicken legs, skin left on
4 cups (1 L) rendered duck fat

Creamed Corn

6 ears fresh local corn
1 shallot, finely diced
1 garlic clove, crushed
4 Tbsp (60 mL) butter
fresh thyme leaves
¼–½ cup (60–125 mL) milk or cream
salt and freshly cracked
    black pepper, to taste

Continued from page 133

Creamed Corn

Begin by scoring corn kernels with a knife, then cutting them off the cob and into a large bowl. Scrape the cobs well to collect all the milky juices in the bowl.

In a saucepan, sautée shallot and garlic in butter for a few minutes. Add thyme and ¼ cup (60 mL) milk or cream and heat through. Add corn and cook, stirring frequently, for 10 minutes.

Creamed corn should be creamy and not too thick. Adjust by adding more milk or cream as needed. Season to taste with salt and pepper.

Chef's tip: Confit preparations originated as a means of preserving meats without refrigeration. For this recipe, duck legs can be substituted for chicken. And if you can't find duck fat, you can use a different cooking oil of your choice.

BEET GREENS

Chicken Soup

DWANE MACISAAC

YIELD: 4–6 servings

Wash and peel all vegetables and then dice to approximately ¼ inch (6 mm).

In a medium-sized heated pot, sauté diced vegetables with olive oil over medium heat. Chop chicken, then add to pot. Toss in bay leaves and herbs. Pour in stock and bring to a boil. Turn heat down and simmer for 15 minutes. Season to taste.

2 carrots

3 celery stalks

2 onions

2 garlic cloves

1 small squash (buttercup or acorn)

1 yam

1 sweet potato

1 Tbsp (15 mL) olive oil

1 whole roasted chicken, skin removed and deboned

2 bay leaves

fresh thyme, tarragon, sage and parsley, finely chopped

8 cups (2 L) chicken stock

sea salt and ground pepper, to taste

Risotto with Chorizo and Acorn Squash

TARA BLACK

Makes 6–8 servings

2 acorn squash, halved and deseeded

3 Tbsp (45 mL) oil, butter or bacon fat
    (bacon fat is the best)

1 onion, chopped

3 garlic cloves, crushed

1 tsp (5 mL) salt

1 tsp (5 mL) ground pepper

2 cups (500 mL) arborio or carnaroli rice

8 cups (2 L) chicken stock, heated
    with 2 cinnamon sticks

4 links dry chorizo sausage, sliced thinly

½ cup (125 mL) shaved hard cheese
    of your choice (try Parmesan)

¼ cup (60 mL) sage leaves, fried
    lightly in oil and gently salted

Place squash halves in a Dutch oven. Cover and bake in the oven at 375°F (190°C) for 1 hour.

Meanwhile, in a large pot over medium heat, sauté onions and garlic in fat until they are soft and have a little colour. Add a little salt and pepper to sweat out the flavours.

Stir in rice and make sure all grains are coated with fat. Over medium-low heat, start ladling warm stock into the rice, about ½ cup (125 mL) at a time, stirring constantly while the liquid is being absorbed. Continue adding stock until all liquid has been used.

Spoon out the cooked flesh of the squash and stir it into the risotto. In a small frying pan, cook chorizo for 3 minutes over low heat and then empty the released oils and meat into the risotto. Season with salt and pepper as needed, to your taste.

Serve risotto with shaved cheese and fried sage leaves on top as a garnish.

FRENCH BREAKFAST RADISHES

Corned Lamb Tongues with Sauce Gribiche

CORY PELAN

YIELD: 6–8 servings, as a main course

1½ cups (375 mL) sea salt

¾ cup (185 mL) brown sugar

4 garlic cloves, crushed

1 Tbsp (15 mL) whole black peppercorns

5 allspice berries

5 juniper berries

1 tsp (5 mL) mustard seeds

1 tsp (5 mL) coriander seeds

1 tsp (5 mL) yellow mustard seeds

½ tsp (2 mL) crushed chilies

2 bay leaves

½ cup (125 mL) soy sauce

15 lamb tongues

In a large pot, heat 12 cups (3 L) water, salt and sugar until dissolved. Add remaining spices and soy sauce. Cool.

Place lamb tongues in a glass or stainless steel dish and pour brine overtop. Weigh down tongues with a dish so they stay completely submerged. Let marinate in the fridge for 7 days, stirring every other day.

To cook, place tongues in a pot and add enough water to just cover. Bring to a low simmer and cook for 1½ hours, or until tender. Remove tongues from pot and peel while still warm. Skin should come off easily. Chill tongues well then slice ¼ inch (6 mm) thick on the diagonal. Arrange on a plate and serve with Sauce Gribiche.

Sauce Gribiche

Serve this sauce with chilled lamb tongues.

Separate egg yolks from whites. In a bowl, mash egg yolks and Dijon mustard together until smooth. While whisking, slowly add olive oil until fully incorporated and emulsified. Add remaining ingredients, including the finely diced egg white, and stir until incorporated.

Chef's tip: A classic combination with the vinegary sauce and full-flavoured yet delicate textured lamb tongue. Any type of tongue will work with this recipe—lamb just happens to be my favourite. Adjust cooking time according to the size of the tongue. Use 2 hours for pork, 3–3.5 hours for beef. Your local butcher should be able to supply lamb tongues with a little notice.

Sauce Gribiche

2 eggs, hard boiled

1 Tbsp (15 mL) Dijon mustard

½ cup (125 mL) olive oil

2 Tbsp (30 mL) white wine vinegar

2 Tbsp (30 mL) chopped fresh parsley

2 Tbsp (30 mL) chopped capers

½ Tbsp (7.5 mL) chopped fresh tarragon

4 Tbsp (60 mL) chopped cornichon (not sweet)

SALT SPRING ISLAND SHEEP

Crème Brûlée Trio

DWANE MACISAAC

YIELD: 6 servings

1 pint (500 mL) fresh raspberries, divided
1 Tbsp (15 mL) ground espresso
2 oz (60 g) quality dark chocolate, chopped
6 large egg yolks
6 Tbsp (90 mL) white sugar
1 vanilla bean, split lengthwise
2 cups (500 mL) whipping cream
12 tsp (60 mL) sugar, for topping
butane torch
6 ¾ cup (80 mL) brûlée dishes

Preheat the oven to 325°F (160°C). Press 6 berries and place on their sides in the dishes. Reserve remaining raspberries for garnish. Add espresso to two dishes and chopped chocolate to the remaining two, leaving two plain.

In a medium bowl, whisk yolks and 6 tablespoons (90 mL) sugar together until blended. Scrape in seeds from vanilla bean and gradually whisk in whipping cream.

Divide mixture among dishes. Arrange dishes in a 13 × 9 × 2-inch (33 × 23 × 5 cm) baking pan and add enough hot water to the pan until it comes halfway up the sides of the dishes.

Bake custards for 30–40 minutes, or until set in the centre. Place the pan on a work surface covered with a dry cloth. Cool custards in pan for 30 minutes. Remove dishes from water and chill unwrapped for at least 2 hours. Sprinkle 2 teaspoons (10 mL) of sugar overtop each one. Torch all custards until sugar just starts to caramelize. Let cool for 1 minute, then serve.

Duck Liver Parfait

PATRICK SIMPSON

YIELD: 6 servings, as an appetizer

Add duck livers to a large glass dish. Pour milk overtop, cover dish and refrigerate overnight. Drain the livers, discarding the milk (unless you feel like playing a funny trick on someone, in which case you should try offering it as strawberry milk—ewwww!)

Preheat the oven to 300°F (150°C). In a frying pan, melt butter and sauté onions and garlic. Deglaze the pan with brandy. (Drink a swig of the brandy yourself.)

Add cream to the pan, reducing for 1–2 minutes. Let cool while you purée livers thoroughly in a food processor. Add cooled cream mixture, curry powder, salt and pepper, and blend. Strain the mixture through a fine sieve. Do not force lumps through the sieve (the lumps are veins, sinew and other gross stuff).

Pour strained mixture into a non-stick terrine or loaf pan (alternately, you can line the pan with plastic wrap) and place in a bain marie (a hot water bath).

Bake for 90 minutes. Remove parfait from bain marie and cool for several hours or overnight in the fridge.

Unmold by dipping the pan in hot water briefly and then running a clean knife around the edges. Invert onto a plate and serve with cornichons, grainy mustard and toast.

1½ lb (750 g) duck livers

milk, enough to cover livers

2 Tbsp (30 mL) butter

1 small onion, minced

1–2 garlic cloves, minced

¼ cup (60 mL) brandy

⅓ cup (80 mL) heavy cream

1 tsp (5 mL) curry powder

1 tsp (5 mL) salt

½ tsp (2 mL) ground black pepper

Eggs Basquaise

CHRISTABEL PADMORE

YIELD: 3–4 servings

2 red bell peppers
5–6 Tbsp (75–90 mL) olive oil, divided
1 cup (250 mL) yellow onion, diced
2 garlic cloves
4 roma tomatoes
1 medium chili, de-seeded and de-veined
1 tsp (5 mL) small hot dry chilies, minced
½ cup (125 mL) dry white wine
salt and pepper, to taste
½ tsp (2 mL) smoked paprika
2 Tbsp (30 mL) white vinegar
4–6 free-range duck or chicken eggs
6–8 slices dry-cured ham
flat-leaf parsley, for garnishing
baguette, for serving

Preheat the oven to 400°F (200°C).

Place red peppers in a pie plate, with 3–4 tablespoons (45–60 mL) of the olive oil. Place peppers in the oven. Remove after skin is charred.

Dice onions, tomatoes and red peppers and mince chilies and garlic. Warm a frying pan over medium heat, then add 2 tablespoons (30 mL) of the olive oil. Add onions, garlic and chilies and sauté until onions become translucent. Add paprika, tomatoes and peppers and sauté until tomatoes are soft. Add wine and ½ cup (125 mL) water. Stir and cook for 5–8 minutes, or until the mixture is thick and everything is very soft. Remove from heat. Using a hand blender or food processor, blend until the mixture is smooth but still retains some of its original texture. Set sauce aside but keep warm.

In a saucepan, bring 3 quarts (3 L) water to a boil. Add vinegar. Reduce heat to a simmer and carefully break eggs into the water. Poach until yolk is at desired firmness. Remove from water with a slotted spoon and drain on paper towels.

Serve eggs on a bed of warm sauce and garnish with ham and parsley. Serve with sliced baguette.

GARLIC AND EGGS

BILLY & MA

Goat Cheese Cheesecake

DWANE MACISAAC

YIELD: 12 servings

Preheat the oven to 350°F (180°C).

Stir all of the crust ingredients together in a large bowl. Butter a 9-inch (23 cm) spring-form pan. Press the crumb mixture onto the bottom and about halfway up the sides of the pan. Set aside and prepare the filling.

In the bowl of an electric mixer, beat the cream cheese and goat cheese together using the paddle attachment until light and fluffy. Add the crème fraîche and beat to combine. Add the eggs one at a time, beating after each addition, until thoroughly combined. Beat in the sugar and vanilla until combined.

Pour the filling into the prepared crust. Place on a baking sheet and bake in the preheated oven for 55–60 minutes. Rotate the baking sheet halfway through the cooking process. If the cheesecake starts to darken, tent the spring-form pan with aluminum foil.

Remove the cheesecake from the oven and let it cool completely before serving (it will continue to set as it cools). It is best to refrigerate overnight before serving. Run a knife around the outside of the cake, release the form and remove. Cut the cake into 12 wedges and serve.

Crust

2 cups (500 mL) graham cracker crumbs

6 Tbsp (90 mL) melted butter, plus extra butter for the pan

1 cup (250 mL) ground hazelnuts

¼ cup (60 mL) white sugar

Filling

2 8-oz (500 g) packages of cream cheese, at room temperature

12 oz (375 g) log of goat cheese

12 oz (355 mL) crème fraîche or sour cream

4 eggs

1 cup (250 mL) white sugar

2 tsp (10 mL) vanilla extract

Lamb and Nappa Cabbage

TARA BLACK

YIELD: 6 servings, as an appetizer

2 cups (500 mL) rice
1 nappa cabbage
1 Tbsp (15 mL) olive oil
1 lb (500 g) ground lamb
3 Tbsp (45 mL) Dijon mustard
salt and pepper, to taste
2 Tbsp (30 mL) yogourt
1 Tbsp (15 mL) Indian curry paste
2 Tbsp (30 mL) rice wine vinegar

Depending on the variety of rice you are using, steam rice accordingly.

Meanwhile, steam cabbage leaves for 30 seconds, until just wilted, then place in cold water and drain fully, so the leaves are "dry." Set aside and prepare the lamb.

Heat oil in a frying pan until hot, then add ground lamb and brown. Stir in mustard and season with salt and pepper to your liking. Drain lamb mixture on paper towels to soak up excess oil.

In a bowl, mix together the yogourt, curry paste and vinegar to make a sauce.

Place cabbage leaves, lamb, drizzling sauce and rice on a platter and make up bites at will.

ORGANIC GARLIC AND SCAPES

Meatloaf

JAMES MCCLELLAN

YIELD: 4 servings

1½ lb (750 g) Quist Farms lean ground beef

1 egg

2 strips Whole Beast bacon, chopped

½ cup (125 mL) tangy barbecue sauce

2 cloves Salt Spring Island garlic,
    roasted and crushed

1 oz (30 g) crumbled Moonstruck
    Beddis Blue cheese

1 cup (250 mL) Panko breadcrumbs

salt and pepper, to taste

Preheat the oven to 350°F (180°C).

In a large bowl, combine all the ingredients. Season with salt and pepper to taste, then place in a lightly greased 5 × 9-inch (12 × 23 cm) loaf pan, or hand-form into a loaf shape and place in a lightly greased 9 × 13-inch (23 × 33 cm) baking dish. Bake for approximately 1 hour.

Poached Duck Eggs with Morels and Fingerling Potatoes

DWANE MACISAAC

YIELD: 6 servings

In a 5-quart (5 L) saucepan, bring fingerling potatoes to a boil in salted water. Turn the heat down to medium and cook for 10 minutes. Strain and set aside in a covered bowl for later.

In a small saucepan, simmer morels in 2 cups (500 mL) water (or stock) for 10 minutes. Strain and set aside.

In the same pot used for the potatoes, bring the vinegar and 12 cups (3 L) water to a boil. (Turn the heat down to help keep the egg whites intact.)

In a frying pan over medium heat, sweat the butter and shallots. Add the potatoes and morels and sauté for 5 minutes. Cover and set aside.

Crack eggs into a small bowl or ramekin and then add them to the simmering water one at a time. Once all 6 eggs have been added, let cook for 2–3 minutes and then remove with a slotted spoon and set aside on a large plate.

On a large platter for family service, or on individual plates, arrange the potatoes and morels. Place the duck egg(s) on top and drizzle with truffle oil. Garnish with chive flowers or fresh herbs.

2 lb (1 kg) red or white fingerling potatoes
3 oz (100 g) dried morel mushrooms
2 Tbsp (30 mL) white vinegar
2 Tbsp (30 mL) butter
2 shallots, finely diced
6 farm fresh duck eggs
truffle oil, for finishing (optional)
6 flowering chives for garnish

BUBBLE STATION - ISLAND CHEFS' COLLABORATIVE FOOD FESTIVAL

Pork Belly Confit with Preserved Lemon Vinaigrette

CORY PELAN

YIELD: 15 servings as an appetizer, or 10 servings as a main dish

Confit

5 lb (2.2 kg) pork belly, skin removed

4 garlic cloves, minced

4 Tbsp (60 mL) sea salt

**3 Tbsp (45 mL) coarsely
    ground black pepper**

2 sprigs fresh rosemary

2 sprigs fresh thyme

4 bay leaves, crushed

zest of 2 lemons

1 cup (250 mL) freshly pressed apple juice

dry white wine, enough to cover pork belly

**16 cups (4 L) rendered duck fat,
    warmed to a pourable consistency**

Rinse and pat dry pork belly, then rub with garlic, salt, black pepper, rosemary, thyme, bay leaves and lemon zest. Lay flat in a baking dish. Pour apple juice and enough white wine overtop to just cover the meat. Refrigerate for 24 hours.

The next day, remove the belly from the marinade and pat dry.

Preheat the oven to 250°F (120°C). Place belly in a clean baking dish and cover with melted duck fat. Bake for 2–3 hours, or until fork-tender. Remove from the oven and refrigerate overnight in fat. When ready to serve, cut into squares and sauté until crispy in a hot pan, or better yet, deep-fry until golden brown. Serve over mustard greens with Preserved Lemon Vinaigrette.

Preserved Lemon Vinaigrette

In a large stainless steel bowl, mix together the first 5 ingredients. Then, using a hand blender or whisk, slowly add the olive oil.

Serve this dressing with Pork Belly Confit and mustard greens. You can find preserved lemons at better delis, specialty food stores and Mediterranean markets. Use only the rind of the lemon in this recipe.

Chef's tip: Absolutely decadent and irresistible, this dish is best served with company in order to save yourself from eating it all. Most artisan butchers will supply pork bellies and rendered duck fat with a little notice. Ask them to trim the belly as for bacon and you will get a nice square piece that will fit well into a baking dish.

Vinaigrette

¼ cup (60 mL) lemon juice

½ cup (125 mL) white wine vinegar

2 Tbsp (30 mL) preserved lemon rind, lightly rinsed and diced fine

1 tsp (5 tsp) honey

pinch of ground black pepper

¾ cup (185 mL) extra-virgin olive oil

Grilled, Brined Pork Chops with Potato, Yam & Corn Hash and Ginger Peach Chutney

MATT RISSLING

YIELD: 4 servings

In a large baking dish, combine all the brine ingredients except the pork chops and mix well. Place pork chops into the brine, cover and allow to sit refrigerated for 12 hours, or overnight.

Remove pork chops from brine and pay dry with paper towels. Allow pork to come to room temperature before grilling.

Grill pork chops over medium-high heat until 150°F (65.5°C) internal temperature is reached, about 7 minutes per side. Let rest for 5 minutes before serving.

To serve, divide Potato, Yam & Corn Hash among four dinner plates and top each one with a pork chop. Garnish with Ginger Peach Chutney and fresh arugula or watercress or a sprig of fresh rosemary. Using a tablespoon, drizzle cooled Balsamic Syrup around the plate.

Ginger Peach Chutney

Bring a large pot of water to a boil. Score an X into the bottom of each peach, and blanch for 30 seconds. Remove peaches and place immediately into ice water for 2 minutes. The skins should slide off easily.

Continued on page 160

Brine

8 cups (2 L) water

1 carrot, peeled and diced

1 yellow onion, peeled and diced

1 stalk celery, diced

1 sprig fresh rosemary,
     or ½ tsp (2 mL) dried

2 whole cloves

1 bay leaf

⅛ cup (30 mL) brown sugar

⅛ cup (30 mL) coarse salt

4 8-oz (250 g) pork chops,
     bone in or out (your choice)

Chutney

4 fresh peaches

1 garlic clove

1 shallot (or ¼ cup [60 mL] minced onion)

½ jalapeno pepper

½ tsp (2 mL) fresh ginger

1 tsp (5 mL) canola oil

½ cup (125 mL) apple cider vinegar

½ cup (125 mL) honey, or more

1 Tbsp (15 mL) chopped fresh mint

pinch of salt, or to taste

Hash

2 large Yukon Gold potatoes, peeled and cubed

1 small yam, peeled and cubed

4 Tbsp (60 mL) olive oil

½ tsp (2 mL) chopped fresh rosemary

½ tsp (2 mL) chopped fresh thyme

½ cup (125 mL) corn kernels, fresh or frozen

Balsamic Syrup

½ cup (125 mL) honey

½ cup (125 mL) balsamic vinegar

Continued from page 159

Halve each peach, removing the pits. Cut the flesh into 1-inch (2.5 cm) dice. If good-quality fresh peaches are unavailable, frozen ones can be substituted. (Simply thaw, and cut to 1-inch [2.5 cm] dice.)

Mince garlic, shallot, jalapeno and ginger.

In a medium-sized saucepan over medium-low heat, sauté garlic, shallot, jalapeno and ginger in canola oil until translucent, about 5 minutes. Add cider vinegar and honey, and cook until syrupy, approximately 7 minutes.

Add peaches and cook for a further 5 minutes, depending on their ripeness. Peaches should be lightly cooked, and not mushy. Transfer to a shallow pan and cool quickly. Add mint when cool, and season to taste with salt and more honey if needed.

Potato, Yam & Corn Hash

Preheat the oven to 350°F (180°C).

Combine all ingredients except the corn and roast in a single layer on an ungreased baking tray for about 15 minutes, or until tender and beginning to brown.

Add corn kernels and roast for a further 7–10 minutes, or until potatoes are fully cooked.

Balsamic Syrup

In a small saucepan over medium-low heat, combine the two ingredients and cook until syrupy, approximately 10 minutes. Cool.

ISLAND CHEFS' COLLABORATIVE SUPPORTERS

Pork Terrine

MATT RISSLING

YIELD: 8–10 servings, as an appetizer

½ lb (250 g) chicken livers,
    soaked and cleaned

2½ lb (1.25 kg) pork shoulder,
    trimmed and diced

¼ cup (60 mL) minced shallot

2 garlic cloves, minced

½ cup (125 mL) heavy cream

2 eggs, lightly beaten

3 Tbsp (45 mL) flour

2 Tbsp (30 mL) brandy

salt and pepper, generous amounts

In a food processor, purée livers and one-third of the pork meat until smooth. Empty into a large bowl and pulse remaining pork meat until coarse.

Add remaining ingredients to the bowl and mix. Place into a lined terrine mould and bake in a water bath at 300°F (150°C) until the internal temperature reaches 155°F (68°C), about 1½ hours. Allow to cool before serving.

Roasted Chicken with Roasted Vegetables

DWANE MACISAAC

YIELD: 4–6 servings

Take chicken out of the fridge 30 minutes before it goes into the oven. Preheat the oven to 425°F (220°C).

Peel vegetables and roughly chop them. Break garlic bulb into cloves, leaving cloves unpeeled. Pile all the vegetables and garlic into the middle of a large roasting tray and drizzle with olive oil.

Drizzle chicken with olive oil and season well with salt and pepper, rubbing it all over the bird. Carefully prick lemon all over, using the tip of a sharp knife (if you have a microwave, you could pop the lemon in for 40 seconds at this point, as doing so will really bring out the flavour). Place lemon inside the cavity of chicken with the bunch of herbs. Place chicken on top of vegetables on the roasting tray.

Roast chicken until its internal temperature reaches 180°F (82°C). Baste it halfway through cooking and if vegetables look dry, add a splash of water to the tray to stop them from burning. When cooked, take the tray out of the oven and transfer chicken to a board to rest for 10 minutes before slicing and serving.

2 medium onions

2 carrots

2 stalks celery

1 bulb garlic

3 Tbsp (45 mL) olive oil, plus
    more for chicken

1 whole free-range chicken
    (about 3 lb [1.5 kg])

sea salt and freshly ground black pepper

1 lemon

small bunch of fresh thyme,
    rosemary, bay leaves and sage

HEIRLOOM CARROTS

Roast Lamb with Moroccan Spices

BILL JONES

YIELD: 8 servings

Spice Mix
1 whole dried red chili
2 Tbsp (30 mL) whole coriander seeds
2 Tbsp (30 mL) whole cumin seeds
5 whole allspice berries
1 Tbsp (15 mL) whole black peppercorns
1 Tbsp (15 mL) whole fennel seeds
4 whole cardamom pods
1 Tbsp (15 mL) ground cinnamon
1 Tbsp (15 mL) ground nutmeg

Lamb
1 deboned leg of lamb
    (3–4 lbs [1.5–1.8 kg])
1 Tbsp (15 mL) minced garlic
salt and pepper, to taste
1 Tbsp (15 mL) olive oil
1 cup (250 mL) apple cider

Preheat the oven to 400°F (200°C).

Place leg of lamb in a non-reactive pan and rub it with the spice mix, plus the garlic, salt and pepper. Allow to rest for at least 30 minutes. Tie up the roast (with butcher's twine) or cook it as is.

Rub the skin side with olive oil and give it a good sprinkling of salt and pepper before putting it in the oven. Pour the apple cider and 1 cup (250 mL) water into the pan.

Roast for 45–60 minutes, or until the internal temperature reaches about 130°F (54°C) for medium-rare. Cover the meat with a piece of aluminum foil and allow to sit for at least 10 minutes. Remove any twine and carve into slices.

We use local Cowichan Valley Lamb from a number of excellent producers. We buy whole lambs at around 75 lb (34 kg) for the best yield and mild flavour. The leg from this animal will weigh 3–4 lb (1.5–1.8 kg) and serve up to 8 people. The lamb is great roasted or we will barbecue the leg on our pellet smoker grill for truly amazing results. The Moroccan flavours go nicely with a couscous made with local dried fruit and herbs.

ASTY SALTED PIG PARTS

BOCCALONE

A CHEF'S FOCUS

FIRE-ROASTED CHICKEN

CONTRIBUTORS

Tara Black (ICC Treasurer 2011, 2012) completed her culinary training through North Island College and Vancouver Community College, and has spent the last nineteen years building her career as a pastry chef. She has worked in bakeries and cafés, large wholesale producers and hotels. Past employers in Victoria include the Inn at Laurel Point, Pure Vanilla, Patisserie Daniel and the Fairmont Empress Hotel. Currently she co-owns and operates Origin Gluten-Free Bakery.

Alesha Davies started AJ's Organic Catering in August 2008 because she felt a need to make delicious, healthy, local, organic ingredients more accessible to the public. Promoting the ideas of food security, recycling, and composting right alongside the amazing taste of local, seasonal food, AJ's Organic Café & Catering opened in downtown Victoria in late 2010. Alesha continues to provide quality, sustainable, organic and local foods out of her busy and growing café in the Atrium, while delivering all of that same great food and service to her catering business.

Heidi Fink is an award-winning culinary instructor and food writer, specializing in local foods and ethnic cuisines. Previously the Executive Chef of the renowned restaurant ReBar Modern Food in Victoria, Heidi now shares her cooking expertise and enthusiasm through her classes, food articles and culinary tours. Please visit chefheidifink.com.

Anna Hunt was born into a family big on sharing food, wine and each other's company. She began her professional career in Montreal at the four-star neighbourhood hot spot Taverne sur le square, where she worked for five years before returning to Victoria. In Victoria, she worked at Stage Wine Bar and then Paprika Bistro where she took over the reins after its sale in 2009. Anna stays connected with her roots through her family's business, Victoria Spirits, where she works as a culinary consultant, splashing great food with great gin.

Bill Jones is a chef, author and food consultant living in the Cowichan Valley on Vancouver Island. He is the author of ten cookbooks, his latest being *The Deerholme Mushroom Book* (Touchwood, 2013). His farm dinners have been profiled in *Gourmet*, *Saveur* and *Harrowsmith* magazines.

Ash Lenick received classical culinary instruction in Toronto, Ontario, where he specialized in Mediterranean and local Canadian cuisine. Currently the Executive Chef at The Hat at the Malahat Mountain Inn, Ash moved to moved to Vancouver Island three years ago in search of Island sustainability, working in the Cowichan Valley.

Dwane MacIsaac (ICC President 2011, 2012) is the Chef/Owner of Passioneat Foods, a farm-to-table catering company. Dwane is also an accomplished chef instructor at Cook Culture, a Victoria culinary hub located in the Atrium building. In January 2012, Dwane was the host of his own cooking show on Chek 6

called *YUM*, which ran for thirteen episodes and featured fellow like-minded chefs from Vancouver Island.

James McClellan (ICC Secretary 2010, 2011, 2012) is the Executive Chef and Director of Food Services at Shawnigan Lake School. He trained in culinary management at Georgian College in Barrie, Ontario, and apprenticed in Four Seasons Hotels and restaurants in and around Toronto. James worked at the Four Seasons Resort located in Nevis, West Indies, as well as at the Mayflower Inn in Washington, Connecticut. He moved to Vancouver Island in 2002 and was the Executive Chef of the Fireside Grill until 2006. "I've always followed the philosophy of if you don't support your local farmer, who will?"

Cosmo Meens is the co-creator of Mo:lé Restaurant, Café Bliss, the late Village Family Marketplace, and The Hot and Cold Café. Cosmo has been featured in *Western Living*, *Eat Magazine*, *Boulevard*, *Monday Magazine*, the *Vancouver Sun*, *Vancouver Cooks 2.0* and the *Times Colonist*. He has travelled to Hawaii and Arizona, working in raw food retreats, as well as being the Executive Sous-Chef at the

Raw Spirit Festival in Sedona, Arizona, two years in a row. He travelled to Beijing with the Canadian Olympic triathlon team as their chef for the 2008 Summer Olympics. Cosmo currently works with his wife, Leah Meens, at The Hot and Cold Café. He is also offering regular cooking classes at Cook Culture

David Mincey (ICC past president) is the Executive Chef and co-owner of Camille's Restaurant, a fixture on the Vancouver Island fine dining scene for over twenty-three years. In 1999, David and five other local chefs formed the Island Chefs' Collaborative and he has been instrumental in designing and implementing many of the ICC's most notable ventures, including the Farmer Grant Program and the Bastion Square Farmers' Market. David was honoured to serve as the ICC president for three consecutive years. In addition to Camille's, he and his wife, Paige Robinson, run Preservation Foods, a company that produces a full line of canned goods, all sourced from Island farms, and imports North America's finest selection of artisanal chocolate.

Christabel Padmore (ICC Vice President 2011, 2012), is the co-owner and chef of Little

Piggy Catering and previously Little Piggy Bakery and Chuleta Restaurant. Christabel received her Red Seal in 2006, having worked as a culinary instructor, restaurant and catering cook since 1994. She attributes much of her culinary inspirations to her mum, her husband, holidays to her family's home in the Auvergne region of France and time spent studying and travelling in the Middle East and Asia.

Michael Pagnacco studied culinary management at Algonquin College in Ottawa, where he graduated with honours. Michael joined Fairmont Hotels and Resorts in 1999, first working at The Fairmont Château Laurier, then moving to The Fairmont Château Whistler in 2000. At the Wine Room at the Château Whistler, Michael's culinary philosophy and passion reflected the growing trend towards a healthier and down-to-earth lifestyle. Michael then left Canada in search of international exposure, first at the Fairmont Dubai, then in Abu Dhabi. Michael returned to Canada in January 2012, joining the historic Fairmont Empress Hotel as the Executive Sous-Chef.

Cory Pelan (ICC Past President and Treasurer) received his culinary training at Vancouver

Community College over seventeen years ago. He is currently the owner of The Whole Beast Artisan Salumeria in Oak Bay and works as a freelance chef/consultant. Cory is passionate about, and dedicated to, the cause of sustainable food production on Vancouver Island. He is also a member of Slow Food Canada and was on the steering committee for the 2010 Canadian Chefs' Congress. When he's not working, he can be found tending to his garden at home and spending time with his wife and nine-year-old daughter.

Jonathan Pulkner learned on the job, working at some of Victoria's finest establishments. He apprenticed at Camille's Restaurant and completed his Red Seal. Today, he works as a food consultant and private caterer featuring traditional barbecue. He was on the Vancouver Island organizing committee for the Canadian Chefs' Congress event that took place at Providence Farm in Duncan in the fall of 2010. A long way from his first job at the CNE carnival, he has come full circle by opening his own food truck, The Refiner Diner.

Matthew Rissling, like many cooks and chefs of his generation, grew up watching cooking shows on PBS, tuning in to see stars like Julia Child, Graham Kerr, Jacques Pepin, Jeff Smith, and of course James Barber on the CBC. Also, the un-fussy cooking styles of his mom and aunts proved to be lasting influences. Matthew earned his Red Seal in 2004 and has continued to move on with his career, earning the position of Executive Chef at the Marina Restaurant in May 2009. Matt lives in a small footprint with his wife, daughter and son in Saanich.

Garrett Schack learned his love of wholesome good food and strong work ethic while living in Germany as a teenager. Fifteen years ago, love brought him to Victoria, where he continued on his cooking path, working at several local eateries around town. Garrett attended Camosun College and completed his Red Seal designation. He went on to travel the world, experiencing different cultures, which is now reflected in his cooking. Garrett took the reins at Chateau Victoria in 2007, helping to revive Clive's into a vibrant cocktail lounge and ensure that Vista 18 Restaurant continues to grow as a premier place to dine in Victoria.

Patrick Simpson is the co-owner and chef of Little Piggy Catering and previously Little

Piggy Bakery and Chuleta Restaurant. Patrick attended culinary school at Malaspina College in Nanaimo and completed his apprenticeship with Delta Hotels in Kananaskis, Alberta. He then went on to work as a chef in Britain, Scotland and Australia, before returning to Vancouver Island where he worked at the Coast and Marriott hotels in Victoria.

Paul Stewart studied at the Stratford Chefs School, graduating with honours. He then went on to complete his apprenticeship and Red Seal certification. His food philosophy is fresh, local and seasonal and he prides himself on cultivating excellent working relationships with farmers, growers and purveyors in various Canadian regions. Now living in Victoria, Paul is pursuing catering and consulting opportunities.

John Waller began his culinary training under the austere tutelage of acclaimed chefs such as Mark McEwan and George McNeil. His career brought him to the bounty of the West Coast as he began to define his own signature style, falling in love with the Cowichan Valley. He previously held the position of Executive Chef at Tofino's Wickaninnish Inn and is currently the chef at the Oak Bay Bistro.

INDEX

ACKNOWLEDGMENTS

Thank you to:

Christabel Padmore for coordinating the cookbook project for over three years and bringing the project from concept to print;

Maryanne Carmack and Hunt and Gather for their generous contributions of photography;

Tara Black and Jason Found for their contributions to the Cookbook Committee;

As well as the following people for their assistance with writing and editing material:

Anna Hunt

Matt Rissling

Ceri Barlow

Justine Wardle

Julita Traylen

Ryann Salik

Sarah Thornton

Don Genova